FOLLOWING JESUS

Following Jesus

A Disciple's Guide to Luke and Acts

WILLIAM KURZ, S.J.

CHARIS

SERVANT PUBLICATIONS
ANN ARBOR, MICHIGAN

Charis Books is an imprint of Servant Publications especially designed to
serve Roman Catholics.

Servant Publications—Mission Statement
We are dedicated to publishing books that spread the gospel of Jesus
Christ, help Christians to live in accordance with that gospel, promote
renewal in the church, and bear witness to Christian unity.

Servant Publications
P.O. Box 8617
Ann Arbor, MI 48107
www.servantpub.com

Cover design: Steve Eames

03 04 05 06 10 9 8 7 6 5 4 3 2 1

Printed in the United States of America
ISBN 1-56955-378-5

Library of Congress Cataloging-in-Publication Data

Kurz, William S., 1939-
  Following Jesus : a disciple's guide to Luke and Acts / William Kurz.
    p. cm.
  ISBN 1-56955-378-5 (alk. paper)
  1. Christian life--Biblical teaching. 2. Bible. N.T. Luke--Criticism,
interpretation, etc. 3. Bible. N.T. Acts--Criticism, interpretation,
etc. I. Title.
  BS2595.6.C48K87 2003
  226.4'06--dc22

                                                          2003015055

Contents

Contents

Introduction

How to Understand and Apply Scripture

Jesus is alive! He is present with us still, as he was present to his disciples in Galilee. Just as his Father pitched his tent among the Israelites in the Old Testament, and Jesus walked with the apostles in the New, so he dwells among us today in our cities, suburbs, and homes—if we but open ourselves to his presence. He is present through his Holy Spirit who lives within us. He is present to us in his sacraments, especially the Eucharist. He is also present to us in Scripture, God's inspired Word to us.

The Gospel of Luke, the Acts of the Apostles (also by Luke), and the other Scriptures contain the living words of Jesus, God and man, who is as near to us today as our next thought. Through these Scriptures, Jesus calls each of us personally to walk the path of discipleship, instructing us by his example and teachings.

From my own experience as a teacher, Scripture scholar, and priest, I am convinced that the messages in Luke and Acts remain important for today. They are not historical relics to be excavated, classified, and placed in a museum. They are not quaint tales that we occasionally consult for nostalgia's sake. Nor are they curious dead specimens, to be dissected like some exotic species.

The stories and parables in Luke and Acts are meant as models and examples of the way in which a Christian will walk in any era. They continue to guide us through the theological confusion and complex issues of life in the twenty-first century while they tell what happened to Jesus and his disciples. For this reason, it is important to *read* the Scripture references cited in this book. The sayings of Jesus in Luke and the speeches of the disciples in Acts seek to explain the meaning of events in everyday life to believers of any age who walk in this Christian way.

Listeners and readers in the ancient world regarded most stories as examples for living, whether they were historical, biographical, or fictional. Thus, through the recounting of the Passover story, Jews identified with the original Israelites being freed from slavery in Egypt. The New Testament writers used their Greek Old Testament the same way.

The manna in the desert is echoed in the Lord's Prayer: Give us *this day our daily bread*. The Exodus wanderings in the desert were models for following the Lord Jesus on the Christian way. First Corinthians 10:1-13 interprets the crossing of the Red Sea and the water in the desert as a lesson for Christians. Just as those Israelites could not presume on God's special calling and care for them if they did not obey him, so Christians cannot presume on their baptism and Eucharist if they put the Lord to the test as did the Israelites.

Authors fashioned even historical stories with an eye to helping readers identify with and imitate historical persons in past events. Thus, Luke's description of Stephen's death in Acts 7 calls attention to its close parallels with Jesus' death. Whereas Jesus says, "Father, forgive them; for they know not what they do" (Lk 23:34), Stephen requests, "Lord, do not hold this sin against them" (Acts 7:60). To Jesus' prayer, "Father, into thy hands I commit my spirit" (Lk 23:46), corresponds Stephen's,

"Lord Jesus, receive my spirit" (Acts 7:59). Both these deaths are models for how Luke's readers should respond when they come to face death.

The truth of a story as an example for imitation does not depend on whether or not it took place. The parable of the Good Samaritan is fiction, but, at the end of the story, the lawyer is told (and the readers through him) to go and do like-wise (Lk 10:37). The book of Jonah is similarly fictional, but in Luke 11:29-32, Jesus uses the repentance of the Ninevites at the preaching of Jonah as an example that his own listeners should follow.

The use of biblical narratives as examples for contemporary Christian imitation is a perfectly legitimate application of Scripture. It respects the way in which the Scriptures were in fact written and used by both the Jews and the first Christians. We will follow this approach as we search out the Christian way of living in Luke and Acts.

Unfortunately, some modern-day uses of the Scriptures do not respect the way in which they were written or intended to be used. Approaches that go from modern issues to Scripture can abuse the intent of God's revelation in his Word. They tend to isolate texts in the Bible that pertain to the issue, rather than reading the text on its own terms and in its full context.

There are two common abuses along these lines. "Proof-text-ing" takes passages out of context to solve questions that they were not meant to answer. Proof-texting has been a common practice in many different Christian traditions. For example, Acts 8:14-17 has been used to prove either that a second recep-tion of the Spirit beyond baptism is necessary, or that the stand-alone sacrament of confirmation existed in the first century.

A second common contemporary abuse is to gather all the texts that explicitly refer to a particular question in order to explain each passage away, to make a case that they are not authoritative for the contemporary issue. For example, some argue that prohibitions against homosexuality in the Old Testament were actually against practices connected with idol worship and therefore do not pertain to the gay movement today. Others claim that certain texts are culturally conditioned and therefore no longer apply.

Arguments that "prove" that Scripture does not condemn homosexual actions overlook overwhelming New Testament emphasis that God intends sexual union exclusively for the context of family and marriage. They also ignore the overwhelming evidence of the practice of the early church, as well as the revulsion of both Jews and Christians toward widespread homosexual practices in their Greco-Roman environment. Instead of such special pleading, we need a more honest approach to searching the Scriptures.

We should steep ourselves in God's Word through frequently reading and praying it. We should seek to know God's ways and his thoughts. We try to put on the mind of Christ. Then, when issues arise, deep-rooted and habitual familiarity with the Scriptures enables us easily to find Christian responses to them within the overall context of how God deals with humans.

The great Fathers of the church such as St. Augustine steeped themselves in God's Word in this way, and allowed it to shape their attitudes. They taught Scripture on a pastoral as well as on an intellectual level, so that the Scripture came alive. Faith and holiness were required of a Scripture teacher in addition to intellectual training. The patristic approach to teaching

Scripture had three characteristics: it was *personal*, *practical*, and *transparent*.

Their teaching was powerful because it was *personal*. The Fathers did not just lecture on abstract or historical levels. They spoke from their personal experience of the realities to which the text was referring. They showed the way in which they had personally come to know God's love, forgiveness, revelation, and power. They also addressed the personal experience of their listeners. They treated and presented Scripture as God's Word, not only to people who lived long ago, but also to all who read it in any age.

The Fathers' approach to teaching Scripture was also *practical*. They did not teach as academic scholars in a university who have no relationship to the lives of their students outside the classroom. They were bishops, catechists, and teachers in a local church. They were pastorally involved with the lives of those to whom they taught the Bible. They used the Scriptures to teach their congregations how to relate to God and to one another. They found in it examples of good and bad behavior.

Finally, the Fathers' teaching was *transparent*. They witnessed freely to their own faith and love and did not hide behind their scholarship, as so many university professors today. They shared themselves as well as their ideas with those they taught.

In this book, we shall try to follow the lead of the Fathers in approaching and teaching a biblical text. We shall investigate Luke and Acts in their own setting and context, and insert ourselves into the journey with Jesus and his disciples to discover the Christian way for our own lives today.

The phrase "Bible teaching" describes this special approach

to elucidating Scripture. It looks not just at what a text originally meant, but what it means as God's Word to us today. It is based on sound understanding of Scripture and of church doctrine, and applies this understanding to our lives.[1]

The scholarly and academic approach to Scripture is important for understanding what a book or passage actually says. It clarifies when, where, and why it was written, the meaning of the book as a whole, the literary forms it used, and the original meaning of the words. It shows us the meaning the passage had for its original readers.

This historical-critical approach is necessary as a check against interpreting Scripture in an anachronistic fashion that reads our contemporary viewpoints back into Scripture and thus misunderstands and abuses it. In my university graduate courses, I devote much of my time to laying historical critical foundations for interpretation. Nevertheless, many scholars and writers are convinced that more than just historical criticism is necessary.

Bible teaching responds to the need for a way of getting beyond scholarly results and applying Scripture directly to life.[2] In contrast to historical criticism, the power of Bible teaching comes from the teacher's personal witness and conviction. Bible teaching is more similar to patristic teaching than to the mere academic presentation of facts and theories.

It does not merely impart knowledge about Scripture, but helps Scripture transform the hearers' lives. It also teaches Scripture as God's inspired and living word addressed to the whole church. It treats an individual book as part of the whole canonical Bible and God's total revelation. Therefore, other parts of the Bible can illustrate the point of the passage under discussion.[3]

Bible teaching also approaches Scripture as the church's book. It functions within the broader context of church teaching, including dogmatic and sacramental teaching in their appropriate Scriptural contexts.[4] For example, John's prologue about God and the Word can introduce a supplementary teaching about the Trinity and the historical development of the doctrine of the Trinity up to its definition at the Council of Nicea in A.D. 325.

Bible teaching of this sort is especially critical for Catholics. Few Catholics who become excited about Scripture have access to such teaching. The approach in their parish Scripture teachings or in academic courses continues to tend to be overly historical, critical, and uninspiring.

However, the teaching at Bible churches, which some Catholics find far more inspirational than what they receive in their own parishes, is often problematic. Such churches often use non-Catholic traditions to interpret Scripture. They may subject Catholics to criticisms of Catholic practices and beliefs. Such inspirational but non-Catholic Bible teaching often results in Catholics losing their faith.

Non-Catholic Bible teaching is often individualistic—it proceeds on the supposition that the church has little or nothing to do with interpreting Scripture. All that the individual needs is Jesus and the Bible. Such approaches are incompatible with Catholic practice and teaching.

They are even incompatible with the way in which the New Testament came to be written—by church leaders and apostles, for the church and within the church. Before the invention of the printing press in the 1400s, it was impossible even to talk about the Bible and Jesus without the church, because most

Christians were unable to have their own copies of Scripture. The only way in which most Christians learned the Bible was by hearing it in their churches. The individualism of so many non-Catholic "Bible teachings" that Catholics attend makes inspirational but Catholic Bible teaching an urgent need, a need that has persisted from the eighties to today.

This book will try to respond to that need by presenting personal and pastoral Bible teaching with reference to what Luke and Acts show us about following Jesus. This second edition will reaffirm the insights of the first that have stood the test of time and make whatever adjustments are required for developments from the 1980s to our situation at the beginning of the third millennium.[5]

ONE

The Basic Themes of Luke and Acts

Before we plunge into Bible teaching, it will help to consider the details of specific passages, certain basic themes, and the organization of the material in Luke and Acts, for the same author wrote both Luke and Acts as Volumes 1 and 2.

A pervasive theme in Luke and Acts is that *discipleship is a life journey with Jesus.* God does not intend us to live like atoms in random motion; we are called to follow Jesus in a definite direction, toward the Father. When Jesus calls us, we do not know all the different roads we will be taking, although at times he may tell us our further destinations through prophecies or promises. We have to stick close to Jesus to avoid getting lost. Like Jesus, we have to get directions for our journey from praying and listening to our Father and from following the Holy Spirit's guidance.

Jesus invites each one of us to follow him on the Christian way. He reaches out to us wherever we are, even in sinful situations, and calls us by name. He asks us to leave behind whatever has been keeping us away from him so that we might follow him.

Another of Luke's themes is that to follow Jesus on his journey means that *we need to face our fears.* We need to trust the Lord and live one day at a time. In the roughly twenty years between the first and the current writings of this book, the utter centrality of trust in God and of living one day at a time has become clearer to me than ever. We must also be realistic about the cost of discipleship and be willing to pay it. For Jesus does not tread a path of glory, but enters glory through suffering and death. We can only follow Jesus in the direction he is heading, toward Jerusalem, where he will go up to the Father through suffering and death.

Repeatedly, Luke demonstrates that Jesus came not to be served but to serve. Therefore, to follow him we also need the heart of a servant. We must learn to get our minds off our selves and our own desires, for we can do only what we are told. We let go of anxious thoughts, for God whom we serve will take care of the ultimate results. We only work for him. We do not focus on ourselves and on our own advancement but on those whom Jesus asks us to serve. All who follow Jesus have to learn to die to self.

We look to Jesus and his disciples in Luke and Acts for examples to imitate on our own journeys with Jesus. We imitate not by wooden mimicry of words and actions, but by letting Jesus' example inspire us toward similar attitudes and approaches in whatever situations in which we find ourselves. As we look at what Jesus did and said, we try to have the same mind in us that was in Christ Jesus (Phil 2:5). Thus do we learn how to behave like Christ in our Christian journey.

Our own power is not adequate for us to rely upon for the journey. Luke lets us know that *the Holy Spirit empowers us for the Christian way.* Through the Spirit we are enabled to do signs and wonders that heal and attract others to Christ. God provides the power and resources needed for our journey, as he did the manna for the Israelites in the desert.

Nor may we simply go our own way or follow our own caprice and plans. We permit the Holy Spirit to show us where to go and what to undertake. In preference to asking God to help us with our projects, we invite the Holy Spirit to lead us into cooperating with what God is doing in the world. In that way, as Luke puts it, the Word of God will increase, and God's salvation shall reach to the ends of the earth. The Christian way is guided by the Spirit.

God offers his Holy Spirit to all humans, not only to a select few prophets and kings as in the Old Testament. For these times in which we now live with Jesus are the final days when God's promises are being fulfilled. God has poured out his Spirit on all flesh as he promised in Joel 2:28-32.

Jesus calls us not simply so that we can find personal happiness. He asks us to spread the good news and bring others along on the Christian way. He encourages us to reach out to all peoples and classes, for God wants all of us to know him as Father. God wants to pour out his Spirit on *all* flesh.

God's Initiating Love—Luke 1–2

God begins our Christian way. Even before we are born, he prepares the circumstances for us to follow Jesus.

Luke demonstrates that God has a plan for each of our lives. In his providence, God provides the situations in which he wants us to love and serve him. At critical moments, he personally intervenes, both in history and in our own lives, to set that plan in motion. Before he sends us forth on our adult mission, he usually prepares us for it in secret. In our hidden lives we have a chance to grow and mature before our mission becomes public and we are exposed to the counterattacks of God's enemies.

No matter how improbable our mission may look, nothing is impossible with God. His power levels mountains, fills in valleys, and makes rough ways smooth (cf. Is 40). We need not fear that opportunities we lacked, poor family backgrounds, or limitations in talents or resources will thwart his plan for our lives. After all, God makes sterile women pregnant and raises the dead to life. Can he not also overcome our shortcomings and difficulties?

These beliefs directly contradict some of the most pervasive worldviews today. The world at large does not believe in a God who repeatedly intervenes in history or in our personal lives. Many contemporary thinkers, including some theologians and Scripture scholars, have adopted this worldview, consciously or not.

Deism has influenced western thought since the eighteenth-century Enlightenment. Popularly described, deism posits that God created the world with natural laws to run on its own, as a watchmaker, who makes a watch, winds it up, and lets it run. Just as the watchmaker does not keep opening the watch to interfere with its running, God does not interfere with the natural forces he has set in motion. Deism rules out miracles and special revelation. There is no point in asking God to do anything to change a problem. At best, we can pray only for the strength to bear with the situation. Generally, we are on our own in this world and we have to make the best of it.

This leads to a popular beatitude: "Blessed are those who do not expect anything, for they shall not be disappointed." This deistic attitude contradicts the Christian way as Luke and Acts describe it. From the very beginning of his Gospel, Luke confirms us in our belief that God plans for and intervenes in our lives.

When we say we see God's intervention in some event, we are making a faith statement. What some people describe as coincidence we understand as an answer to prayer. It takes faith to see God's plan at work in our lives, and, generally, we only see that plan in retrospect.

It is sometimes especially hard for new converts to realize that God has been working in their lives even before their conversion, preparing for it. St. Augustine was one who did recognize this. He commenced his *Confessions* not with his conversion but with his conception. Though he admitted to God, "Late have I loved thee," he praised God for caring for him from the very beginning of his life. In retrospect, he could see God's plan for his life in a way that he could not when he was going through the events he recounted.

The first two chapters of Luke's Gospel show how God similarly prepared the way for his Son, Jesus. The chapters are likewise written in retrospect. They look backward from Jesus' ministry to select the important people and aspects of his infancy that illustrate how God had been preparing for that ministry.

Every situation speaks of God's initiating love. In Luke 1–2, angels are the most frequent signs of that intervention. God unexpectedly intervenes on behalf of Zechariah, an old priest married to a barren woman, Elizabeth. Through Gabriel, God announces the birth of a son, John, who is to go before the Messiah to prepare a people to receive him (Lk 1:5-17). Through Gabriel again, God speaks to a virgin named Mary, asking her to bear his Son. He assures her that nothing is impossible to him, as the sterile Elizabeth's pregnancy attests.

God's plan for his Son depends on Mary's free "Yes" to that plan. God initiates, but he waits for our cooperation with his plan. Because Mary did say yes unconditionally, the Holy Spirit came upon her and created God's Son within her womb, opening the door to our salvation. She continued to say yes, as when

Simeon predicted her pain (Lk 2:34-35), and especially at the foot of the cross (Jn 19).

God's ways are unpredictable. The most important person in the world for our salvation, after Jesus himself, was a young girl in Nazareth betrothed to a carpenter. Mary's song of praise in Luke 1:46-55 beautifully summarizes God's way of saving us. It echoes similar songs of thanksgiving for God's salvation in the Old Testament, especially that of Hannah (1 Sm 2), and bears witness to the constancy of God's love. With Mary, we praise God because he has looked on our lowliness and blessed us beyond expectation. She shows us how gracefully to acknowledge God's gifts that people see in us, and yet to direct their praise to God.

In their barrenness, Elizabeth and Hannah appreciated their dependence on God. When they finally became pregnant they did not boast. They recognized their conceiving as a powerful sign of God's power intervening in their lives. The sign of Mary's conceiving by the Spirit alone was even more remarkable. All these women embody one of Paul's most basic messages: God demonstrates his power in our human weakness (2 Cor 12:9).

The song of praise of Zechariah, the father of John the Baptist, blesses God for keeping his promises made ages ago to Abraham. His promises do not always come true when we expect. However, Scripture repeatedly demonstrates that in due course God is faithful to his word.

John's calling is ours as well: to "go before the Lord to prepare his ways, to give knowledge of salvation to his people in the forgiveness of their sins, through the tender mercy of our God" (Lk 1:76-78). Although John preceded Jesus, Jesus was the greater one to whom he pointed.

Luke 1–2 portrays Jesus' greatness as hidden from the world and perceived only in faith. With all his majesty Jesus was born to lowly parents in wretched circumstances because "there was no place for them at the inn." God works even through the frustrations of the poor. Our assurance of God's providence does not spare us disappointments in life.

Simeon's prophecy in Luke 2:29-35 assures us that God has planned what is happening to Jesus as his way of saving many. It also warns us that Jesus will be a sign that is contradicted. He will be the occasion of the downfall of those who reject him and of the rise of those who accept him.

In these mixed responses, the thoughts of many hearts stand revealed as people react to Jesus and to us his followers. This "prophecy of doom" gives hope at the same time that it sobers us to prepare for hardship. Surgeons warn prospective patients for open-heart surgery that they will experience extreme pain. Nevertheless, they also assure the patients that if they exercise in spite of the pain, they will soon be healthier than they have been in years. This kind of "scientific prophecy" helps patients to endure pain with hope. Simeon's prophecy likewise can keep us from becoming dismayed when disaster strikes.

Luke 1–2 presents another very important pattern for our Christian way. Jesus lived a hidden life at Nazareth for about thirty years before beginning his brief mission. Meanwhile, he "grew and became strong, filled with wisdom; and the favor of God was upon him" (2:40). After a brief foretaste of his future ministry, the boy Jesus went back into obscurity for eighteen more years. He "increased in wisdom and in stature, and in favor with God and man" (2:52).

All of us as individuals and as groups need time to grow and mature before being plunged into ministry. We can make little practice forays into ministry immediately after conversion, but being a servant of God takes depth and maturity. It took time even for Jesus; it takes time for us. Many rush into service before they are ready, and are unable to handle the problems that arise. They end up discouraged and "burned out," their promise for genuine service lost.

We need obscurity and freedom from the expectations of others so that God can get our lives in order and strengthen us to serve and to bear authentic fruit. The Jesuit training I went through involved fourteen years of hidden study away from exposure to the ordinary world. My only forays into ministry were three years of teaching as a seminarian before my theology studies. When I finally began my "public life" of teaching, I had matured beyond my first fumbling attempts at ministry.

What is true for individuals I have also experienced as applicable to groups. As a member of a small prayer community, I realized how a new group of lay Christians generally needs time to grow and become strong before attempting outreach. Our small lay community came into being as an offshoot from a larger charismatic prayer group. I have always been quite grateful that so few people knew of its existence in its first few years.

Our initial "hidden life" gave us time to grow in prayer, to establish strong committed relationships, and to correct major flaws in the way in which we had lived. It gave us an opportunity to develop skills for leadership and service. As we have become more mature, God could make better use of us, both as individuals and as a group, to serve other believers and the church.

The Call of Jesus at the Jordan—Luke 3–4

Even before our Christian way begins, we have all had our personal salvation histories. God has begun working in our lives from the very moment of our conception. As babes in the womb, we can be frightened by harsh noises or soothed by loving sounds. The pace of our experiences picks up when we come forth from the womb. Certain experiences stand out more than others do. Many that we do not even recall continue to influence us unconsciously. When we talk about our own lives, we tend to select those stories that mean the most to our listeners. We may choose to vary the points in our lives at which we begin our story; at times we proceed chronologically, at times in some other logical order.

Writing about Jesus, Luke made similar decisions about which events to stress, which to omit. When he did not know the chronological order of the narratives and sayings he had gathered from diverse sources, he selected some other principle of order. Luke organized much of his miscellaneous material into the setting of Jesus' journey to Jerusalem.

Sometimes Luke changes the order he found in Mark's Gospel, which most scholars consider was one of his sources. For example, he moves the Nazareth speech to the beginning of Jesus' ministry in his own account from its setting in the middle of Mark's Gospel. In Mark, Jesus discusses the great commandment in a hostile situation in Jerusalem. Luke made that commandment part of Jesus' instructions to his disciples on their journey to Jerusalem (Lk 10:25-28). In these modifications, Luke was not acting as a purely secular historian. He had pastoral purposes in writing his Gospel and Acts. He wrote from his faith to provide his readers with Christian models to follow.

By placing the great commandment within the intimacy of Jesus' journey with his disciples, Luke emphasizes the total love for God and neighbor with which we should live as Christians. He further illustrates the meaning of this commandment by the narratives he places after it—the Good Samaritan and Martha and Mary. Finally, the Lord's Prayer sums up love of both God and neighbor (10:29–11:4).

As we review our lives, many of us recognize major datable turning points, times when we experience the Holy Spirit commissioning us in a special way. A major early turning point for me took place in the summer of 1969. I was to be ordained deacon that fall and priest in the following summer of 1970.

I realized that I lacked a good deal of what I needed if I hoped to be an effective priest. At an earlier student retreat in which I had helped as a seminarian, all I had been able to contribute was a kind of "pop psychology." It seemed obvious to me that if I was going to offer psychology, I should become a professional psychologist, not a priest acting as an amateur one. People do not need "pop psychology" from priests: they need the powerful preaching of God's Word. They need God's sacramental power to help and heal them. At that time, I simply did not have the strong faith conviction and authority to preach that I would need as a deacon.

In my search for something more, I visited a prayer meeting at Visitation Academy in St. Louis, where a friend had been prayed over and had been transformed from a cynic to a believer. Despite my aversion to some of the things the group did, I hungered for the power and experience of God I could see they enjoyed. I longed to experience personally the power of the Holy Spirit to enable me to touch souls as a priest.

When I was able to surrender my own ideas about how to do

things, God overwhelmed me with his love. That love was so overpowering that I was confident that he wanted me to be a priest. The experience was like an ecstatic honeymoon with God that lasted for two entire weeks. I no longer wondered about his presence in my prayer; I could now speak about God with conviction. I now had something to give as a priest. This experience was a datable turning point in my life, and even decades later I remember vividly the people who were present and the place where it happened.

A similar datable turning point changed Jesus' life and began his active mission of preaching. Luke situates it decisively in the context of world history, naming those who were ruling the Roman Empire and Palestine at that time. As the Word of God had come to the prophet Jeremiah during the reign of certain kings (Jer 1:1-3), so it also came to John the Baptist under particular rulers. God breaks into history in sending his word to his prophets.

Just as the charismatic movement of God's Spirit provided the occasion for my turning point, so the Baptist's movement at the Jordan did for Jesus. At the beginning of his mission, Jesus experienced the Father's love and the Spirit's power, in a way I can appreciate more because of my own experience. When Jesus was praying after his baptism, God sent his Holy Spirit upon him and commissioned him: "Thou art my beloved Son; with thee I am well pleased" (Lk 3:22).

Before this, Jesus had been working inconspicuously as a carpenter. Now he began his prophetic mission of preaching and healing. More than any of the other Gospels, Luke emphasizes the role of the Spirit in getting Jesus started on his mission. The Holy Spirit likewise begins every Christian walk or journey with Jesus.

Jesus still did not rush into ministry. First, the Holy Spirit led him into the desert to fast and to sort out in prayer just what his mission was and how he was to exercise it. Luke 4:1-13 relates how the devil tested Jesus' mission as Son of God during those forty days. When we experience the Holy Spirit in new and powerful ways, we also often encounter the evil one. Evil spirits, who could afford to ignore us before, now set to work to deflect us from our true mission.

Therefore, when we open ourselves to the Holy Spirit, we need to learn to distinguish among different spirits. We need to learn whether the promptings we feel or ideas we receive come from God, from ourselves, or from evil spirits. Even Jesus did this after he received the Holy Spirit. He took a time of quiet to distinguish between temptations and his true call as Messiah and Son of God.

The devil first tempts Jesus as Son of God, challenging him to provide for his own needs by changing stones into bread, and, thereby, to control his own destiny. The biggest obstacle against God's ability to use us as his instruments is our own insistence on retaining control. We want to use power and privilege to provide our own security. When we find our lives out of our control, we become anxious and complain against God as the Israelites under Moses had done in the desert.

Jesus refuses to act like the Israelites. He lets go his own control: "Man does not live by bread alone" (Dt 8:3). Later, Jesus will feed the people in the desert with his power as Son (Lk 9:12-17), but now he refuses to act independently of his Father and to provide for himself.

In the second test of Jesus as Son of God, the devil promised him power if Jesus would worship him. Satan's claim to be able to give secular power to whomever he wills sounded plausible.

Many Jews believed that until God's kingdom came, the devil had temporary control over worldly power. Thus, in Revelation 13, the dragon (Satan) gives his power to the beast (Rome). In earlier ages, God's son Israel had repeatedly succumbed to this temptation by worshipping the golden calf in the desert, and by adoring the gods of their powerful neighbors to gain worldly power.

Jesus defends himself against this temptation by means of the teaching of Scripture: "It is written, 'You shall worship the Lord your God, and him only shall you serve'" (Lk 4:8; Dt 6:13). Only if we immerse ourselves in Scripture and its attitudes can we hope to remember God's ways even when tempted in the desert.

Satan can also use Scripture to tempt us under the guise of good, once his more blatant temptations have failed. He appeals to religious enthusiasm to force God's hand and to move ahead of where God would like us to be. In the third temptation, Satan appeals to God's promises of protection in Psalm 91:11-12. He challenges Jesus' belief in this promise in Scripture by asking him to throw himself down from the temple.

Jesus sees through this false appeal to religious enthusiasm and quotes another Scripture in response. We are not to put our God to the test, as the Israelites in the desert had done all too often. The obedient Son, Jesus, submits his life and ministry entirely to the authority of God's word in Scripture as properly interpreted. By doing this, he shows us how to overcome the devil's attempts to sidetrack us. He shows us the danger of trying to keep control over God's power and gifts, of trying to use worldly power as a shortcut to spiritual success, and of rushing ahead of God's will for us by reading biblical texts out of context.

When the devil senses defeat, he withdraws "until an opportune time" (Lk 4:13). This reminds us not to become overconfident when we have overcome temptation. Other tests will come at times when we are more vulnerable than we now are. Thus, the devil waits until just before Jesus' passion. On the Mount of Olives, when Jesus is afraid of his impending suffering, the devil tries again to get Jesus to follow his own will instead of his Father's (Lk 22:39-46). Yet, Jesus remains obedient.

Jesus' genealogy, mentioned just before the temptation account, had referred to Adam as "son of God" (Lk 3:38). In contrast to earlier disobedient sons of God, Adam and Israel, Jesus grounds his ministry as Son of God solidly on obedience to his Father. He thus provides a positive model for us.

As Christian ministers, we are extremely vulnerable if we lack a firm grounding in obedience to God, which alone can keep us from being led astray by the devil, the world, or the flesh. For example, some priests have lost powerful ministries of preaching and healing when they became worn out and discouraged by lack of rest and sensible limits to their ministry. Others have fallen into sin and left the active ministry. The only way we can avoid such tragedies is by obeying God, as his will for us is tested and confirmed by Scripture and church authority and by openness to wise brothers and sisters with whom we relate closely. Those who work alone without accountability or companionship make easy targets for the attacks of God's enemies.

Jesus Outlines His Mission and Way—Luke 4:16-30

As we have mentioned, Luke moves Jesus' speech at Nazareth to the beginning of Jesus' ministry so that it will function as his "inaugural address." Referring to Isaiah 61:1 and 58:6, Jesus presents the results of his discernment in the desert about what his mission should be as Son of God and Messiah: "The Spirit of the Lord is upon me, because he has anointed me." "Christ" in the Greek—or "Messiah" in Hebrew—means "anointed."

Jesus is the Christ or Messiah sent to preach good news to the poor. The poor, not being self-sufficient, long for someone to save them; they find in Jesus an answer to their longings. Jesus proclaims release to captives of Satan through exorcism. He brings sight to the blind, and many other kinds of physical healing. He sends forth with forgiveness those oppressed by sin and guilt. He has come to announce "the acceptable time ... the day of salvation" (2 Cor 6:2).

Jesus has come with the good news of a full salvation. He provides evidence of this good news by concrete signs he works in our lives. He heals us, frees us from spiritual oppression, and forgives our sins. All we have to do is to accept him and let him save us.

Nevertheless, the people of Nazareth do not allow him to save them, for he does not match their expectations. How can a carpenter who made their tables be their Messiah, especially someone who dares to mention salvation even for the Gentiles? They foreshadow his passion by trying to take him out of the city to kill him.

TWO

The Call and Mission of Jesus' Followers

We have reflected on the grounding of the Christian way in the call and mission of Jesus, and on how Luke 1–2 shows God at work preparing for that call even before Jesus' conception. This chapter will consider how the call and mission of Jesus' followers (both in Luke-Acts and today) set them on the Christian way.

The Call of Peter—Luke 5:1-11

Luke 5:1-11 describes the call of Peter in a way that not only describes that event, but lets Christians see themselves being similarly called by Jesus. Because Luke wants us to identify with Peter, he describes Peter's call as a *typical* call to follow Jesus.

Peter is one with whom it is easy to identify because he is so ordinary. He is not rich, or even overly successful as a fisherman! Working on his initiative alone, Peter fishes all night without success. Success beyond his wildest dreams comes only when he obeys Jesus and focuses his work as Jesus directs him.

Jesus asks Peter to obey him even though that seems foolish. After all, Peter, as a fisherman, should know more than a carpenter about how or where to fish. He had already been fishing during the night, the best time, and he had already washed his nets, which would get dirty again if he put them back in the water. But he does obey this person who had been teaching the people from his boat. The huge catch that almost sinks both boats overwhelms Peter. Like Peter, we too find ourselves repeatedly surprised by how rewarding obedience to God can be.

Peter goes through much more than merely amazement. He experiences deep awe at the goodness and power he encounters in Jesus, as well as a feeling of personal unworthiness. Our reaction tends to be like Peter's: "Depart from me, for I am a sinful man, O Lord" (5:8). As with Peter and many of the prophets, many of us ask Jesus not to get too close. Our sense of unworthiness, even "uncleanness," makes us fear the holiness of God, which cannot tolerate the unclean in its presence.

Thus when the Lord calls Isaiah, he cries, "Woe is me! For I am lost; for I am a man of unclean lips ... for my eyes have seen the King, the Lord of hosts" (Is 6:5). The Lord does not deny that Isaiah is unclean. He does not lie to Isaiah out of compassion to make him feel good. Instead, he *cleanses* Isaiah: "Behold, this has touched your lips; your guilt is taken away, and your sin forgiven" (Is 6:7).

How different is God's compassion in responding to our sense of guilt and unworthiness from so many contemporary attempts at compassion. Today, many consider psychological freedom from feelings of guilt more essential than the unpleasant truth that can lead the sinner to seek release from his or her sinful situation and state. In contrast, God does not deny our guilt out of mistaken compassion. God accepts our acknowledgement of guilt and unworthiness, and frees us from that guilt by forgiving our transgression.

Psychology can be helpful in cases of false guilt, a neurotic state where someone feels guilty even though he or she has done nothing wrong. Often, however, the reason that we experience guilt is that we did do something wrong. Denying such healthy guilt solves nothing. Only forgiveness frees from guilt, and we cannot be forgiven if we do not accept that forgiveness by admitting that we need it. Even in human relationships, we know how frustrating it is to want to forgive people who hurt us, but who insist they did nothing wrong. They reject our forgiveness because to accept it would require admission of guilt on their part.

So too with God: we must admit our wrongdoing if we want to experience his forgiveness (cf. Ps 32:3-5). For Catholics, this involves returning to personal practice of the sacrament of reconciliation, in which each person names his or her own sins openly and unambiguously to the church's representative, the priest. In my own life, sacramental confession has been very important in preserving my relationship with God even when other aspects of my prayer life were deficient.

As both penitent and confessor, I can witness to the healing assurance of forgiveness spoken by the confessor in the person of Christ and delegated by the church "in the name of the Father, and of the Son, and of the Holy Spirit." Peter's sense of unworthiness focuses not just on his person but also on his being Jesus' companion, called by him. This reaction, too, he shares with the prophets when they receive their call, and with Christians when we are called to minister to God's people. For who is worthy to speak for God? Who is worthy to be a minister of healing, or to care for God's people? Jesus reassures us as he did Peter, "Do not be afraid; henceforth you will be catching men" (Lk 5:10). We do not need to be perfect, only open to God's forgiveness and guidance, as was Peter.

Like Peter, *every* Christian is called to bring others to Christ. Peter's call, however, required him to abandon his occupation as a fisherman (Lk 5:11). Whether or not God calls us to leave our present occupations, we must be *willing* to follow Peter's example of abandoning everything.

Luke 5 tells us more about Peter's call than do the parallel passages in Mark and Matthew. There we find only the invitations to Peter and Andrew, James and John to become fishers of men (Mk 1:17; Mt 4:19). Extra Lukan details about the miraculous catch and Peter's sense of unworthiness illustrate Luke's emphasis on what makes the story even more directly a model for our own Christian call to follow Jesus. Luke makes it easier for us to identify our own experience with that of Peter. Yet all three versions point out the central mission of a disciple of Jesus: to gather people into God's kingdom.

An especially exciting event early in my university teaching exemplifies this fundamental call of a disciple to gather others to Christ, to evangelize. A nun with a powerful gift of evangelism spoke to my class about the power of the Holy Spirit. After the class, three male students experienced an infilling of the Holy Spirit and spoke in tongues.

They were so excited about their newly experienced reality of God that they shared what happened with roommates, girlfriends, and others in the class. They related how the knee of one of the men, injured in a football accident, was healed when Sister led the rest of us in praying over him. He ran several miles on it later that evening. They brought others to see this nun, to hear the good news and experience it in their own lives.

In less than two months, by the end of the spring semester, at a time when students are usually preoccupied with exams, more than thirty students had experienced the power of the Spirit. Their faith became deeper. I was truly amazed at how God had anointed some of these students with a powerful gift for evangelizing fellow students.

They even showed a sensitivity that kept them from turning people off by pushiness or over-enthusiasm. The foundation they then laid resulted in a student prayer group that lasted more than ten years after the original students had graduated. When Jesus, through his Spirit, empowered and called these students in a new way, he also made them "fishers of men."

The Call of Levi

Luke provides the call of Levi as his next example of our call to discipleship (Lk 5:27-32). He keeps the narrative of this call as uncomplicated as possible: Jesus saw Levi at the tax table and told him, "Follow me." Levi left everything and followed him. Since Luke gives no other details, all the focus is on Levi's immediate response to Jesus' call.

It is very important to follow Jesus when he calls us. Failing to act or to choose is itself a choice. If Levi had remained behind to "discern" whether that call really was for him, that itself would have been a choice. In fact, he would not have followed Jesus. Instead, Levi left everything, and his life was completely different from then on.

This report shocked Jewish listeners because Levi was a hated tax collector, a collaborator with the Romans who made his living by extorting for himself extra money beyond the already oppressive Roman taxes. In Luke 19, Zacchaeus the tax collector indirectly admitted he had cheated and extorted: "If I have defrauded any one of anything, I restore it fourfold" (19:8). The only way in which the Romans could get members of subject peoples to collect Roman taxes from their compatriots was to allow them a free hand in keeping an extra charge for themselves.

Understandably, ordinary people detested tax collectors, but Jesus went out of his way to call one of them. He went to Levi; Levi did not go to him. Levi was still at his unsavory task of collecting Roman taxes when Jesus called him. When Jesus calls sinners, however, his compassion does not include tolerating their sin. Instead, he frees them from their sinful pattern or situation. Authentic compassion does not allow people to perish in their sin, but liberates them from it, enabling them to live God's way in peace and joy. Tolerance is necessary in a pluralistic society to avoid witch hunts and to preserve secular freedoms, but it must not be confused with Christian compassion.

Jesus' compassion for Levi changed him from a hated outcast to a member of Jesus' inner circle of disciples. Levi, too, became a "fisher of men." He did not keep his good news to himself, but invited many other tax collectors, sinners, and other outcasts to a great feast at his house. He wanted to share Jesus with them too. When people first experience God's love and forgiveness, they get so excited that they are simply bursting to tell others.

Not everyone approved of Jesus' associating with such riffraff. Pharisees and the scribes of their party, noted for priding themselves on their righteousness, challenged Jesus' disciples. In the Middle East, eating with someone represented a special form of intimacy. Jesus and his disciples were associating in this intimate way with people whom no self-respecting person would befriend.

Jesus' response to the Pharisees is the same as his response to the self-righteous of any age: "The healthy do not need a doctor; sick people do. I have not come to call the righteous, but sinners to repentance" (Lk 5:31-32). If we, in turn, are to be like Jesus our model, then we too must not be ashamed of associating with "undesirables," no matter what others say.

Luke emphasizes the fact that God feeds the hungry and raises up the lowly; those who are full do not experience any need for God. When Jesus reaches out for disciples, he asks not the respectable Pharisees, but tax collectors like Levi. To be helpful to God as disciples, we must remember our need for God. We never stop saying, "God, be merciful to me a sinner" (Lk 18:13). When we reach out to call sinners to repentance, we do so as fellow sinners who have ourselves been forgiven.

The Call of the Twelve

Though Jesus called many other disciples besides Peter and Levi, Luke lets these two accounts suffice as models for our Christian call. In Luke 6:12-16, however, he shows us a particular call within the more inclusive call to discipleship. Jesus selects the twelve from among his many disciples. They were to have a special role not shared by the others.

Because this decision was so consequential, Luke emphasizes that Jesus prayed all night. He took considerable time to ask his Father "Who are the twelve you want?" He did not choose only the most popular or talented, just as in the Old Testament God had not chosen the most likely of Jesse's sons to be king, but the youngest, David (1 Sm 16:6-12). Roles in a Christian church or community are not to depend on personal dignity or prominence, seniority, or amount of service. According to this example, roles in a Christian group depend entirely on whomever God chooses.

Luke simply calls the twelve "apostles," which means "sent

out." All the lists name Simon first, along with his brother Andrew. Although Andrew is one of the first disciples Jesus called, Luke-Acts does not mention him outside of the lists of the twelve here and in Acts 1:13. Andrew's example illustrates how the earliest converts in a group do not necessarily exercise its most important functions. Christian groups need to beware of the "cult of the original members or leaders," and be open to endorsing new leaders from among later members (like Paul, who did not even know the earthly Jesus).

Jesus renames Simon. Though most Christians refer to him by his Greek name Peter, the meaning of that name—"Rock"—designates his function in the Christian church. Jesus changes his name and responsibility from Simon the fisherman to Rock the fisher of men. Yet this involves more than a name change—the person is also changed. The fearful Peter who denied knowing Jesus became, at Pentecost, the stable leader of his restored people.

Even if he does not change our names, Jesus changes us too when he calls us. He enables us to do whatever he asks of us. God does not focus on our present weakness but on what he will enable us to become and to do. He called Abraham "father of many nations" long before he had his first son, and called Peter "Rock" long before the reliability the name implies was visible in his behavior. When Jesus calls us, he assures us of his hope for what we can become.

What does this pattern suggest regarding Jesus' choice of Judas the traitor? Jesus had spent all night in prayer until God showed him whom to pick, and one of those chosen later betrayed him! Jesus did not make a mistake. God did choose Judas and meant him to rule one of the twelve tribes of Israel (Lk 22:29-30). However, like all disciples, Judas was free to reject his call—in his instance, he did. Though early Christians were shocked that Judas betrayed Jesus, hindsight demonstrates that God used Judas' freely chosen betrayal to bring about Jesus' secret arrest when his popularity would have prevented the authorities from arresting him publicly. Jesus' arrest, enabled by Judas's betrayal, eventually led to our own liberation.

By hindsight, we can recognize similar patterns in our own lives of how God works for the best even in negative circumstances. Once I became ill with a fever, immediately after the semester ended, and had to stay in bed for three days before my scheduled retreat could get underway. At the time, this sickness was most unpleasant.

Though I prayed often for healing so that I could start my retreat, God did not seem to answer my prayers. I started the retreat a day late, and dragged through its first day or two. Still, looking back, I can appreciate how hyperactive I had been just before the retreat. It would have been very difficult for me to be calm enough to pay attention to the important changes God was to ask of me at the retreat, if he had not used my sickness to force me to become quiet before the retreat began.

The number twelve has important symbolism. Jesus chose the twelve to head the twelve tribes of Israel, even though the twelve tribes had not existed as a unity since Solomon's death in 922 B.C. At that time, they split into the northern kingdom, Israel, with ten tribes and the southern kingdom, Judah, with two tribes. In 721 B.C., Assyria destroyed the northern kingdom and the "ten lost tribes" never came together again in any numbers. Jews at the time of Jesus longed for reunion of the full twelve tribes, and prophecies promised this would happen in the end times when God came to establish his kingdom. By choosing the twelve for the twelve tribes, Jesus performed a prophetic sign of hope for the full restoration of God's people.

This hope and longing for reunion of God's divided people provides an important example for today's divisions within Christianity. By choosing the twelve, Jesus indicated his expectation that God's people would be one unified people in God's kingdom. Division is not God's will. The Father wants us to long for unity, to pray for it, and to work for it.

The division among Christians has been an enormous scandal to non-Christians. It is Satan's strategy to divide Christians in order to conquer them. Jesus wants "one flock, one shepherd" (Jn 10:16). Just as both northern and southern kingdoms shared the blame for their split, so do all the Christian denominations, as the catechism, echoing Vatican II, admits (*CCC*, 817, *UR* 3 § 1). The choice of the twelve reminds churches today to long for the reunion of God's people into "one, holy, catholic, and apostolic church."

Some Christian groups make the mistake of not training replacements for their founders. Like Moses in the desert, the original leaders find themselves overwhelmed as a group grows. They have to imitate the solution of Moses, who chose seventy elders to receive the Holy Spirit and to help him lead the people (Nm 11:16-30).

From early in his ministry, Jesus provided for his replacements by calling and training disciples, and eventually the twelve, in a special way. Though Jesus himself is the Cornerstone (Lk 20:17-18), he named Simon as the Rock to succeed him, to "strengthen your brethren" (Lk 22:31-32).

He took his disciples along on his journeys, teaching them by word and example.

In Acts 6 the twelve soon imitated Jesus' example of providing further leadership, when they ordained as their helpers the seven, who represented the Greek-speaking minority in the Jerusalem church. Not only are we to replace and add to the original and current church leadership, we are to do so by including new groups and minorities.

Women Disciples—Luke 8:1-3

How many rabbis had women in the group of disciples who traveled around with them? Luke makes special mention of the women who traveled with Jesus' band.

> Soon afterward he went on through cities and villages, preaching and bringing the good news of the kingdom of God. And the twelve were with him, and also some women who had been healed of evil spirits and infirmities: Mary, called Magdalene, from whom seven demons had gone out, and Joanna, the wife of Chuza, Herod's steward, and Susanna, and many others, who provided for them out of their means.
>
> LUKE 8:1-3

These women played an extremely important role in the events relating to Jesus' death and resurrection. They were among the key witnesses to Jesus' death and burial (Lk 23:49). They discovered the empty tomb, and reported it to the eleven disciples (24:1-11). Their contribution to the beginning of Christianity was inestimable.

Their role was most surprising in respect to the time in which Jesus lived. Neither prophets nor rabbis would normally have women among the disciples who traveled with them. Not only did Jesus make the surprising choice of women, but he also chose particularly unlikely women to be among his companions. Mary Magdalene was especially infamous: "from whom seven demons had gone out" (8:2).

Joanna, the wife of Herod's steward, and others of the women apparently had money, from which they supported Jesus' group, as Lydia the businesswoman later did for Paul in Acts 16. Luke thus gives us a striking picture of the Christian way, with both men and women following Jesus on his journey to Jerusalem and the cross. Like the blind beggar in Luke 18:35-43, these women followed Jesus on his way after Jesus had healed them.

The inclusion of women among Jesus' companions provides another important pattern for discipleship. No one is excluded from the possibility of following Jesus. Mary Magdalene went to his tomb at daybreak and discovered it empty. One of the people closest to Jesus (Jn 20:11-18), a prostitute who had had seven demons, she is an extremely important example for Christians. We are never, in Jesus' eyes, unworthy of a close relationship with him, no matter how sinful we may have been.

By healing and forgiving us, Jesus frees and enables us to follow him on his way, even when that way leads to the cross. It is important not to become fixated on healing. Many of us may need healing as we begin our walk with Jesus. Some Christians, however, constantly talk about needing inner healing, and keep asking for more healing sessions and prayers. There comes a point when we have to start walking, even if we still have a limp! If we start moving to follow Jesus as he ministers to others, we will often find ourselves healed as we move.

Mother Teresa did not emphasize inner healing for her sisters because her experience showed her that they often found healing as they served others and got their minds off themselves. Obviously, people seriously ill need healing, for it is almost impossible for them to focus on much else besides their extreme pain. Eventually, however, we have to admit we are healed enough to give to others. If we follow Jesus on the way to the cross, he may heal us from inhibiting illness so that we are now able really to suffer! Freed of the pain and constrictions that close us in on ourselves, we can face the suffering of persecution as we try to follow Jesus in a hostile world.

Luke 8:1-3 provides another lesson about the role of these particular women that is important for the Christian way today. Their roles and duties in Jesus' wandering band of disciples were not to be the leaders, nor does Luke ever say that they preached to the crowds. While this example does not preclude female leadership, these particular women had a supporting role: by providing for the needs of Jesus and the twelve, they enabled them to preach and to carry out their other ministries. That supporting role was as important as other roles that got more attention. If they had not been there, Jesus and the twelve would have had to pause in their ministries to provide for themselves.

Many holy wives and mothers have performed this essential, if hidden, supporting role for their husbands and families. In today's concern not to exclude women from other kinds of service, we must beware of the pendulum swing toward an attitude that degrades the dignity of homemaking wives and mothers. Some women university students have told me that they want most of all to be homemakers, yet they feel guilty about this desire because of the pressure to have an outside career. Many actual homemakers have said the same thing, now that they find themselves in the unappreciated minority.

The Christian way is primarily service, not self-promotion. It is important to seek justice for women; it is important that women should not be stereotyped and prevented from using their gifts as the Lord leads them. It is also important to recognize the value of and the need for supporting roles, for both men and women.

People in supporting roles have equal dignity with those in the limelight. Thus the women in Luke 8:1-3, who remained on Calvary when the male disciples had fled, and who found the empty tomb and brought the good news to the apostles that Jesus was alive, were just as important to the church as the twelve. Yet they were not the leaders of the church.

Christian Discipleship and the Parable of the Sower

Luke introduces the parable of the sower immediately after mentioning the women traveling with Jesus. This parable is a powerful symbol for us as we spread the good news about Jesus and as we hear that news and respond to it.

Palestinian farmers carried their seeds in a fold of their clothing and scattered them in arcs by hand over the ground. Because the farmers could not plant each seed in suitable soil but had to cast it at random over large areas, many seeds were wasted. The parable tells the sower to keep sowing seeds. Worry about those that are wasted could immobilize the planting process. Only if we keep sowing will there be a harvest, and the harvest will be great, despite considerable loss of seeds.

This parable provides a compelling lesson especially for Christians who preach or teach. As a Scripture teacher, I simply cannot become discouraged because some students do not accept or like what I teach. If I try to avoid offending everyone by not speaking the truth gently but boldly, I will have no harvest of new Christians.

All I can do is sow the seeds of God's Word. Some get trodden under or devoured; some land where there is no depth and the sprouts wither away; some get choked by thorns; but some fall on good ground where they will grow and yield a hundredfold. In the same class in which several of my students became excited about Jesus, others considered the course boring. Instead of becoming discouraged by the inevitable few who reject the teaching, I have to rejoice in the hundredfold of those touched by Christ.

Many Christian teachers and preachers face discouragement because so much effort in sowing the seed of God's Word has no immediate result. The sower sees nothing but many seeds that seem dead on the ground where he has sown them. Only later will the fruit be obvious. Growth is so slow that we cannot normally see it except through time-lapse photography.

Teachers and preachers may see only what seem to be many dead seeds in front of them. Still, the seeds they sow may bear fruit months or years later, though they themselves never see the harvest. Even Jesus never saw the results of his preaching in his lifetime on earth. His capture and death seemed to destroy all he had built up; his followers were scattered. He told his disciples that they would reap what others, like the Old Testament prophets and Jesus himself, had sown.

In Acts 2, Peter reaps at Pentecost 3,000 baptisms, which Jesus had sowed by his death and resurrection. A Christian might say something to a stranger on a bus that later leads to a conversion he never hears about. Some parents die before seeing their hopes for their children's salvation fully realized. Even when we do not see the results of our efforts to sow the seed of

God's Word, we must keep sowing in the faith that God will bring about a harvest.

The parable of the sower also helps Jesus explain to his disciples the results of his own preaching. The disciples might have become discouraged at the disappointing response to Jesus. To them, the parable says that Jesus is carrying out his ministry by sowing seed, but that he does not control the results.

The parable of the sower brings to mind the example of the prophet Ezekiel. He refers to himself as a watchman, who has to warn the people how God is offended by their actions (Ez 33:1-9). When we know God's Word, we too have the responsibility to tell it to others and to speak it clearly. If people listen to us, well and good. If they do not, at least we warned them. If we say nothing, we also become responsible when those whom we did not warn are lost.

The parable of the sower puts a grave responsibility on preachers and teachers and parents to tell people unambiguously what actions are offensive to God, even though they fear their listeners might reject their teaching. For example, many young people have gotten themselves into serious trouble because no one clearly warned them that intercourse outside of marriage is gravely wrong.

> Temptations to sin are sure to come; but woe to him by whom they come! It would be better for him if a millstone were hung round his neck and he were cast into the sea, than that he should cause one of these little ones to sin. Take heed to yourselves; if your brother sins, rebuke him, and if he repents, forgive him.
>
> LUKE 17:1-3

The parable itself focuses on the sower, but the explanation of the parable in Luke 8:11-15 takes a more allegorical approach. That is, it takes many elements of the parable and finds equivalents for them, in an X = Y pattern. Thus, the seed is the Word of God and the different kinds of ground are different receptions of that Word. The focus in the explanation is rather on the different ways in which listeners receive God's Word. It asks us, what kind of soil are you for God's Word? What do you do with the message you have heard?

Like an examination of conscience, the explanation of the parable questions us about the various ways in which we might respond to God's Word. Do we hear it but simply not believe it? Even many churchgoers, including sometimes priests and religious, become uneasy as they listen to others talk about a miracle that they claim to have seen or a healing that they received. They change the topic or in some other way simply block such testimony from their minds.

The explanation of this parable asks us, secondly, whether we initially receive God's Word with joy, but lack roots and fall away in time of testing. A third response we may give to the Word is to have it so "choked by the cares and riches and pleasures of life" (Lk 8:14) that it does not mature and bear fruit in our lives. When God asks us for our love, he wants a single-minded love. Yet many of us are so busy and so preoccupied that there is little chance for God to speak to us.

Finally, we can be good soil and receive the Word with generous response, bearing fruit with patient endurance and perseverance in the midst of trials. It takes time for fruit to grow. We cannot be like the little boy so impatient to see the carrot he planted that he keeps pulling it up to see how big it has gotten! We persevere with patience, even though we cannot see our growth or the fruit of our work. The unofficial Catholic community for prayer to which I belong has remained very small, and in everyday living it is hard to perceive growth in myself or in the other members. Still, as I look back over our twenty-some years, I can see remarkable differences in our members. Deep changes and long-range projects take much time and patient perseverance.

Discipleship and the Storm at Sea—Luke 8:22-25

After the parable of the sower, Luke adds further lessons for following Jesus. Luke 8:16-18 tells disciples not to hide their light but to share what they have received, to keep sowing the seed of God's Word. Luke 8:19-21 defines the prerequisite for being in Jesus' family: "My mother and my brethren are those who hear the Word of God and do it" (8:21). In this context, the storm at sea symbolizes the trials that buffet the Christian church.

As the first Christians told and retold the disciples' experiences in the storm at sea, they emphasized those details that provided a lesson for the difficulties facing their own community. Some details recalled Old Testament stories, such as that of the prophet Jonah sleeping through a storm at sea (Jon 1:5). Some alluded to Psalm 107:26-30 and its imagery of salvation from terror at sea:

> They mounted up to heaven, they went down to the depths;
>> their courage melted away in their evil plight;
> they reeled ...
>> and were at their wits' end.
> Then they cried to the Lord in their trouble,

> and he delivered them from their distress;
> he made the storm be still,
>> and the waves of the sea were hushed.
> Then they were glad because they had quiet,
>> and he brought them to their desired haven.

Still the function of the story was primarily to speak to the church's current situation.

From the earliest centuries, Christians identified the boat as a symbol for the church. As we sail in the direction Jesus gives his church, it may seem to us that Jesus is asleep, unaware of our troubles. We cannot understand his silence and apparent lack of concern for the way his church seems to be sinking and about to capsize.

Why does he not do something about false teaching by priests who tell unmarried penitents that sex is natural and that they need not confess such actions? Why does he not do something about the high percentage of divorce in Catholic marriages? Why does he not do something about rich people who call themselves Catholic but keep the poor in grinding poverty that crushes their spirits and demoralizes their faith?

Once we take the importance of committed Christian community seriously and try to build relationships with some depth in the church, we can also find ourselves in storms. It is relatively easy to relate to most people superficially, but community living requires mutual accountability. When it reaches the depth where we are able to correct and rebuke one another in obedience to Scripture, the storm really begins.

In Christian marriage, religious life, and other forms of committed community life, people freely surrender their independence for the unity of mutual interdependence. As mature adults who have their own way of doing things try to become one, there are bound to be conflicts. Frequently repeated and mutual forgiveness is essential for marriage or for any close community living. The more we develop beyond superficial acquaintance, the more we disappoint and hurt one another and the more our faults grate on one another. What may have seemed in the beginning more similar to a romantic cruise can now find itself a ride buffeted by the winds and waves of dissension.

Similarly, in the church, we can find our boat tossed in violent storms that shake us from within and attack us from without. In the midst of these storms, we have no control. Jesus must be asleep, or why would we be in such predicaments? In the Psalms, Israel turned to the Lord pleading with him to wake up, asking how long it would be before he would intervene to help them.

The disciples likewise turn terrified to Jesus: "Master, Master, we are going down." Jesus rebukes the wind and raging waves and they become calm. A major sign of the Holy Spirit, of Jesus' action in our lives, is peace. However, once Jesus has restored calm, he turns to us and asks, "Where is your faith?"

The disciples come to a growing realization of Jesus' identity by the way in which he calms the storm. Similarly, as we experience Jesus rescuing us from impossible crises, our faith in his divinity grows. For who can command the wind and waves but God? No matter how apparently hopeless or terrifying the crises in which our boat finds itself, we must continue to believe that Jesus remains with his church. We turn to him in trust and endure in courageous hope while we wait for him to save us.

The Mission of the Seventy—Luke 10

As we follow Jesus, there will be times when we cannot merely be comfortable with being fed and learning from him. There are times when Jesus sends us on mission apart from his sensible presence. Jesus prepared his disciples for their ministry by sending the twelve and here the seventy disciples on "training missions."

Disciples begin by simply learning from their master. Eventually, however, good teachers or leaders want to prepare others to take their place. Jesus knew his disciples would not be ready for their full mission until the Holy Spirit empowered them at Pentecost, but meanwhile he sent them out to prepare towns for his coming. He delegated small tasks to increase his own effectiveness and to train them. After these missions they would report the results to Jesus so that he could commend them and correct them.

As disciples of Jesus, we need to be ready to leave the comfort of being with Jesus in order to be workers in his harvest. Although an extended period of daily prayer while listening to Jesus is very important, those with directly pastoral missions actually spend most of their day in work. St. Ignatius Loyola was a mystic who could easily spend hours in prayer, but he forbade his Jesuit followers to meditate more than an hour a day so that they could serve the church more actively.

As leaders, we can learn from Jesus' example to delegate responsibility and to train our own replacements. So many powerful ministries are one-man or one-woman productions that disappear after that person is gone. From very early in his ministry, Jesus prepared disciples who could carry on his work and who could reach far beyond his human limitations of time and space.

Good leaders make themselves dispensable. Ministers who are indispensable sometimes cling to the ministry as *theirs*. They should rather be concerned about people beyond the limits of their own time, energy, and even life spans. Jesus' heart went out to the needs of the people not his own: "The harvest is plentiful, but the laborers are few; pray therefore the Lord of the harvest to send out laborers into his harvest" (Lk 10:2).

This training mission was to challenge the disciples. "Go your way; behold, I send you out as lambs in the midst of wolves" (10:3). Jesus sends us out beyond what we can securely control. We are as defenseless as lambs among wolves. We cannot be disciples of Jesus if we are afraid to take risks. This is why Jesus first heals, loves, teaches, and prepares us before giving us high-risk missions.

Peter needed the grace of the coming of the Holy Spirit at Pentecost before he was able to confront 3,000 Jews in Jerusalem and ask them to repent for having Jesus, the Messiah, crucified by pagans (Acts 2:23, 38). When Peter had tried to rush prematurely into defending Jesus during the passion, he failed miserably and three times denied knowing him. Jesus has important and risky missions for many of us, but first he wants to train us and empower us. When Jesus asks us to do something, he empowers us to do whatever he commands us to do.

THREE

Following Jesus in Trusting Our Father—

The previous chapter presented some vivid patterns for discipleship in the parable of the sower and in the accounts of the storm at sea and of the commissioning of the seventy. All of these patterns of discipleship require fervent trust in God. Such trust is a primary theme in Luke's Gospel, especially in the sayings of Jesus. In this chapter, we examine the Lord's Prayer and other sayings that call us to trust in God our Father.

The Lord's Prayer—Luke 11:1-4

Jesus' mission journey began when God called him forth as his beloved Son. When the devil tested his sonship, Jesus remained loyal to his Father. Between God's saying, "You are my beloved Son," and the testing of Jesus as Son comes the genealogy which begins, "Jesus,... being the Son (as was supposed) of Joseph, the son of Heli,..." This genealogy goes up the ladder of ancestors until it arrives at "Adam, the son of God" (Lk 3:23-38).

Therefore, one way in which Jesus was Son of God was as son of Adam. Since we are all descendants of Adam, we are all likewise in some way sons and daughters of God. As God's children, Jesus teaches us to pray to God as our Father.

Jesus is never quoted as saying to his disciples, "Today our lesson will be on how to pray." Jesus apparently lived and traveled with his disciples for some time before they noticed his life of prayer. Out of the desire that Jesus had stirred up in them by his example, they asked him to teach them how to pray. It is a joy to teach a group of people who long to learn how to pray because they have either experienced God themselves or have seen others touched and changed by God. How different from teaching groups, whether classes or congregations, in which many are only present from a sense of obligation.

Further, we cannot effectively teach others how to pray if we do not ourselves pray and know how to pray. We can push abstract concepts around a theological chessboard without personal experience of what we are teaching. Yet if we want to help people actually to pray, we have to pray ourselves.

Then we can share from our own experience what we have learned. The experience of others will not be exactly the same as ours, since prayer is a personal two-way communication with God, and no two people are the same. With no personal experience of prayer, we risk forcing some method of prayer down people's throats, whether or not it fits their personality and needs.

Jesus taught his disciples to pray by using insights from his own human experience of prayer. Even skeptical scholars tell us that we can be historically certain that Jesus called God his Father or "abba." This is how the human Jesus experienced God. He definitely wanted us, as his disciples, also to pray to God as Father.

For the last three decades, some radical feminists have been criticizing the use of the word "Father" or of other masculine terms for God. Some have been trying to change what they call sexist wording in the Bible. Some would rather address God as "Mother."

Such suggested changes are rooted to a certain extent in a laudable desire to eliminate from Scripture negative views toward women. It is also true that God is beyond designation as masculine or feminine, and that Genesis tells us that "God created man in his own image,... male and female he created them" (Gn 1:27). However, often enough these critiques of Scriptural language also stem from an ideology that is foreign to the Bible and that too readily dismisses the authority of the Bible as patriarchal and with a bias against women.

Although Jesus referred to such feminine qualities of God as maternal tenderness, his principal term for God was "Father." Even though in the cultural milieu in which both the Old and New Testaments were written, there were frequent references to goddesses and divine mothers, biblical imagery purposefully focused on God primarily as father and husband. This is the symbolism Jesus himself used and taught us to use.

Thus, in Luke 11, when the disciples ask Jesus to teach them how to pray as John had taught his disciples, Jesus instructs them to address God as he does: "Father, hallowed be thy name. Thy kingdom come. Give us each day our daily bread; and forgive us our sins, for we ourselves forgive every one who is indebted to us; and lead us not into temptation" (11:2-4).

The first question that strikes most Christians who read this is: "Where are the missing words?" The version with which we are familiar is Matthew's, which has "Our Father, who art in heaven ... Thy will be done on earth as it is in heaven.... But deliver us from evil." Although Luke's version is shorter, the meaning is actually quite comparable.

"Father" in Luke 11 implies "Our Father," since the petitions later are to give *us our* bread and forgive *us our* sins. "Thy will be done on earth as it is in heaven" in Matthew's version primarily develops the implications of "Thy kingdom come." Similarly, "But deliver us from evil [the evil one]" parallels and brings out the implications of "and lead us not into temptation."

Parallel complementary sentences of that kind are customary in Hebrew poetry such as the Psalms. Thus, Matthew's Our Father, which churches use today, has the kind of parallelism common to the Hebrew of the Old Testament, to the Aramaic Jesus spoke, and to other related Semitic languages. Luke's version apparently follows instead the Greek tendency to drop repetitions that might sound redundant.

Though not expressed in precisely the same words, the two versions may well be variant versions of the prayer as Jesus taught it on different occasions, or variations in people's memories of the same prayer. Alternatively, each may correspond to the version used in the respective evangelist's church. Jesus is informing us, "God is my Father; I am giving you permission to call and experience him as my Father and as your Father."

What Jesus does not recommend is that we call God, "Almighty Judge." Our stance before God in this life is not primarily one of a defendant before a judge. Neither are we trying to earn heaven by doing good and avoiding evil. Jesus is not even telling us to pray to God primarily as King. He is telling us to pray to God as Father.

In the civilization to which Jesus belonged, the father was a venerable authority figure. A father's authority over his family was extensive and seldom challenged. When, therefore, Jesus instructs us to pray to God as Father, he is telling us to pray to an authority figure. However, the authority is not a judge but a father. Thus Jesus' instructions guide us between the extremes of excessive fear of God and inappropriate familiarity.

Jesus' familiarity with God is that of a son with a loving Father, "Abba." Their relationship is one of deep and intimate love, but it also incorporates obedience to the Father's supreme authority. A loving authority figure is neither a stranger nor adversary nor friend, for a friend is usually an equal and does not have authority over the other.

This portrayal by Jesus of God as Father is consistent with the Old Testament picture of God, though "abba" is a more intimate term than any found in the Old Testament. The Jews did regard and pray to God as their Father. The Old Testament has several places in which God and Israel express intimate love for one another (Ex 4:21-23; Is 43:1-7; Dt 32:5-6).

Jesus restates and emphasizes this Old Testament view of God as Father. Though the Psalms address God in many ways other than as Father, Jesus puts his emphasis on Father, rather than on Yahweh or Lord. He wants us to know that God invites our intimate approach no matter what wrong we have done. Like the father of the Prodigal Son, God is a Father who waits anxiously for our return.

This was exceedingly good news for Luke's readers in the Greco-Roman world. Many Greeks and Romans had quite forbidding views of God. When pagans considered how good people were crushed through no fault of their own, they began to view the gods as arbitrary and sadistic.

In Shakespeare's *King Lear*, whose fictional setting is the ancient world, one of the characters has had his eyes put out and maintains, "We are as flies to the gods. They kill us for their sport." This vivid figure of a child squashing insects at random expresses the helpless fear that many ancient people felt before the arbitrary blows of the gods. They feared to draw too much attention to themselves through success, lest jealous gods should cut them down to size.

It was quite understandable that some Greek philosophers would react against such portrayals of the gods by denying that gods even exist. It is less frightening to be completely on our own in this universe than to be subject to the whim of fickle gods. To these pagan skeptics, Jesus and the early church brought the good news that God is a loving, providing Father, an authority, but a just, not an arbitrary one.

The Structure of the Prayer

The Lord's Prayer is not merely a set prayer to be memorized. It also provides a model of how we are to pray even when we use our own words.

"Father." Jesus teaches us to begin prayer by focusing on God, not on ourselves and our needs. We begin with worship and praise of God. After we call him Father, expressing trust and gratitude and love, we immediately pray, "Hallowed be thy name." That is, may your name be kept holy, may your name be reverenced and praised. This prayer of praise turns to God in worship and praises his holiness. We should begin most prayer with praise, rather than with requests for the things we need.

This praise is a will-act, a choice we make to praise God. It does not depend on our feelings. We may feel tired or distracted or anxious or sick with a headache. We can disregard our own feelings and burdens to focus on God in praise. As we concentrate more and more on God, we often find our feelings gradually changing from anxiety to joy and peace. Thus, Christ blesses us when we follow his example and begin our prayer with "Father, hallowed be thy name," rather than with "Give us every day our daily bread."

"Your kingdom come." This petition asks that God's will be followed and accomplished here on earth as it is in heaven. At the time of Jesus, the Jews longed for God's kingdom to come. When David's kingdom was destroyed and foreign powers dominated them, Jews kept asking when God would establish his kingdom and put an end to pagan oppression. This prayer of Jesus, however, relates to a wider concern.

In the Book of Revelation, the prophet John hungers and thirsts for justice, for vindication. Why are evil people getting richer and the good becoming poorer and more oppressed? Even today, this world does not seem fair. Why does God fail to do anything to redress all its injustices?

The Old Testament had no compelling answer to that question. Job asked where justice was when a just man suffers. God's only answer to him was that Job was not God and could not hope to understand God. Qoheleth (or Ecclesiastes) asks almost cynically where justice or meaning is. Qoheleth wonders whether life is a meaningless cycle: there is a time for everything, for building up and tearing down.

Only at a time closer to that of the New Testament were the Jews intellectually equipped to understand God's revelation that he would bring his kingdom into the world. That would entail a destruction of the present unjust order, followed by a new creation, "the world to come" as the rabbis called it. Whether the focus is on recreating and restoring this world, or on the other-worldly domain of heaven with its eternal life, salvation and the answer to our world's injustice comes not from human effort but from God's rescuing power.

Before people were able to understand a revelation about eternal life in God's new creation, the question of how God could be just in such an unjust world was unsolvable, even in Scripture. One cannot teach nuclear physics to a two-year-old; a toddler's mind simply cannot grasp it. Similarly, God had to wait for the human race to grow in its experience and wisdom before he could reveal his nuanced answer to injustice.

"Your kingdom come" asks for God's answer to injustice,

innocent suffering, and sin in our world. It expresses the desire that God's will be done, that we stop hating and harming one another and begin to behave as God wants us to. "Your kingdom come" is a hunger and thirst for justice, for an end to nuclear arms proliferation, for an end to the millions of abortions, for an end to famine in Africa while Americans fret about being overweight.

"Your kingdom come" implies our cooperation with God in working for justice. Its hope is not in our efforts, however, but in God's establishing his kingdom. We do not "build the kingdom of God on earth," as many seem to believe. Only God can bring his kingdom. Many Jews of the Zealot party rejected Jesus as Messiah because he would have no part in their violent liberation movements.

Jesus' and our prayer is that God may send his kingdom. We must not impatiently take God's justice into our own hands and try to bring relief for economic injustice through violence. In some of his foreign visits, as in one of his early visits to Latin America, Pope John Paul II confronted both unjust rightist regimes with the need for social justice and leftist regimes or activists about their temptation to substitute atheistic Marxism or violent revolution for Christian social justice.

"Give us each day our daily bread." This petition recalls the Old Testament accounts of the manna in the desert during the Exodus from Egypt. God led the people into the desert so that they could learn to trust him to provide for them.

> "And you shall remember all the way which the Lord your God has led you these forty years in the wilderness, that he might humble you, testing you to know what was in your heart, whether you would keep his commandments, or

not. And he humbled you and let you hunger and fed you with manna, which you did not know, nor did your fathers know; that he might make you know that man does not live by bread alone, but that man lives by everything that proceeds out of the mouth of the Lord."

DEUTERONOMY 8:2-3

The first temptation of Jesus in Luke 4 recalls this lesson. One of the biggest tests in the life of all of us is whether we will trust God to meet our needs.

Exodus 16:16-21 recounts the manna incident in a way that stands as lesson for all generations. God commanded the people to take as much of the manna as each one would eat that day. No one was to hoard manna for the next day. The Israelites were to trust that God would provide tomorrow's food tomorrow. Yet the human instinct to hoard is great, so that some people disobeyed. The hoarded manna rotted and bred worms.

"Give us each day our daily bread" recalls this biblical lesson against hoarding. Hoarding causes shortages and deprives the poor of their needs. Hoarding says, "I've got to provide for all possible future needs, because no one else will take care of me. I will take care of myself, and I do not care if there is enough for others. If I do not take this item, someone else will and I will have nothing."

This self-centered attitude results in long lines in a gasoline shortage, as drivers line up just to top off their tank with the last gallon that it will hold. If people hear news of a failure of the peanut crop, they take all the peanut butter from grocery shelves, thus causing an instant shortage. When people hoarded sugar during a shortage of sugar decades ago, sugar prices doubled and tripled and never came back down to a point even close to that of their previous level.

The lesson of the manna is, "Thou shalt not hoard." If you hoard that manna it will rot! All hoarded wealth rots or is at risk of damage or theft. In another saying, Jesus tells us not to store up treasures on earth, where thieves break in and steal or moth and rust consume. Hoarding causes anxiety about the security of our wealth. The Lord's Prayer asks for bread for one day at a time.

Matthew's version makes this point even clearer than that of Luke does. "Give us *this day* our daily bread." We are not even to ask for tomorrow's bread! Rather, we shall ask our Father again tomorrow for the bread we need that day. This is the normal behavior of small children toward their parents. Children come each day for their food and simply trust their parents for the following day's needs. Jesus wants us to be like little children before our heavenly Father with this kind of trust.

Exodus 16:22-30 applies the manna lesson to the Sabbath. Each day we are to gather for our needs, except on the Sabbath. On the sixth day we are to gather for two days, and obey God's command to trust him and to rest and to keep the Sabbath day holy. The manna that is stored for the Sabbath will not rot.

Our contemporary culture has obliterated any Sabbath or Sunday rest. Yet keeping the Lord's day holy is a very important part of biblical religion, and one that we need today, perhaps even more than did earlier generations. We have become such workaholics, so frenetic in our pace. Our busyness leaves little room for our love relationship with our Father.

Keeping the Sabbath is an act of trust. It enables us to devote one day a week to God, allowing him to recreate us as persons, families, churches, and friends. We depend upon God with the confidence that our work on the other six days of the week will provide sufficiently for our needs. The Sabbath is like a tithe of our time to God. Tithing money to God is an extremely important biblical command and a way to trust God with our money. The Sabbath offers us a way to trust God with our time.

"Forgive us our sins, for we also forgive every one who is indebted to us." The second part of this petition is the hard part. Jesus here makes it very clear that when we ask forgiveness, we in turn must be willing to forgive. Matthew's version of the Lord's Prayer stresses this even more explicitly: "Forgive us our debts, *as* we forgive our debtors." Immediately after the prayer, Matthew's Gospel adds the explanation, "For if you forgive men their trespasses, your heavenly Father also will forgive you; but if you do not forgive men their trespasses, neither will your Father forgive your trespasses" (Mt 6:14-15).

All of the above is implied in Luke's version of the prayer, although it is not stated as explicitly. If we do not forgive those who sin against us, we are throwing away the gift of God's forgiveness. All of us have needed forgiveness from God. All of us have been alienated from God from our very conception, and we have added by our own sins to that alienation. To the original sin of Adam and all the other sins of the world, we add our own wrongdoing, for which we need forgiveness.

Forgiveness is at the heart of any love relationship. The people who are closest to us are the ones who can hurt us the most. We take down our defenses for those whose love we accept. We put our trust in them, leaving ourselves vulnerable to betrayal by them. We put our hope in them, so that as a result they can disappoint us. We value their opinion of us, so that their rejection hurts much more than rejection by a stranger. If a stranger offends me, I can often slough off the affront; but when someone I really love offends me, that hurts.

However, to love is impossible if we keep walls around ourselves to protect ourselves from getting hurt. We can keep the walls up, and be miserable with loneliness; or we can take them down, experience love, but also get hurt by those we love. At times, we all disappoint one another. Since it is impossible for us to love without making ourselves vulnerable, love requires a dying to ourselves. We have to be able to forgive when those we love hurt us. If we cannot, we cut off the love relationship and instead put up defensive walls.

We are unable to live a fully human life if we are so afraid of making a mistake that we cannot attempt anything. Neither can we have love relationships if we are so afraid of offending our loved ones and not being forgiven that we cannot be ourselves or relaxed around them. We live with one another in the knowledge that we need to expect both to forgive and to be forgiven daily so that we all can be free. As we know we need forgiveness when we fail, so do those we love. To love our neighbors as ourselves we must forgive them as we ourselves want to be forgiven.

A very serious problem I often discover in my pastoral work is the holding of grudges, sometimes for as long as twenty years! Occasionally, married people tell me that their spouse did something to offend them twenty years ago. My temptation is to respond by saying, "Well, that is your problem now. If you have not forgiven them by now, there is something wrong with you." Grudges have no place in a Christian's life.

If we want to be forgiven, we *have* to forgive. Otherwise, we imprison people in our lack of forgiveness. Someone may have hurt us badly many years ago, but if we do not let them out of the prison of our lack of forgiveness and of our resentment, they remain confined and inhibited. They stay locked in that cell until we let them out. The Lord tells us, "If you want me to forgive you, all I ask is that you do the same for others who hurt you." When we pray his prayer, we ask that the Father's will be done in us so that we can forgive as we ourselves want and need to be forgiven.

"And lead us not into temptation." In his agony in the garden in Luke 22:40 and 46, Jesus twice urges his disciples to pray that they might not enter temptation, that they might not succumb to the test. In the Lord's Prayer we all ask to escape from temptation. In Luke 22:41-44, Jesus models this request for us. He begs to overcome his temptation not to accept the cup of suffering. As a result, he remains strong and does not succumb to the test. By contrast, his disciples give the bad example of failing to pray in time of testing. Jesus "found them sleeping for sorrow" (22:45).

It is so hard to pray when we are depressed. However, because the disciples let their depression keep them from praying, they failed their test. They failed miserably, denying and abandoning the man they loved more than anyone else. So we learn from Jesus to pray often: "and lead us not into temptation."

Thus the Lord's Prayer summarizes our main needs: to know a loving God as Father, to praise God and to pray for his will to be done, to receive from him our daily needs, to forgive and be forgiven, and to be spared from succumbing to the tests in our lives.

Two Parables About Trusting God—Luke 12

In Luke 12, two parables express the strong Lukan theme of trusting in God and not in money. Luke 12:13-21, the parable of the rich man with the extraordinary harvest, introduces Luke 12:22-31, the parable of the lilies and birds.

The first parable describes a rich man who had a huge harvest and asks what he should do with it, for his barns were unable to store all of it. It never seems to have dawned on the man that others might need his extra food. Instead, he decided to build bigger barns to store enough for the rest of his life and never have to work again. However, God said to the man, "Fool! This night your soul is required of you; and the things you have prepared, whose will they be?" (12:20). This statement forces us to consider the loneliness of the rich man. He has no friends, for he has spent his life hoarding for himself.

Many people have their preparations and hopes for the future frustrated. The stock market can fail us. Unexpected sickness or death can prevent the enjoyment of savings that have been accumulated over a long period. The fundamental truth about the lives of all of us is that there is no such thing as earthly security. Luke and Jesus teach that we depend totally on God. We cannot even predict how long we will be alive.

An image came to me in my thirty-day retreat that vividly expresses the reality of our situation before God. I remembered how a friend of mine was throwing his baby daughter up in the air, and how much she loved this experience. My friend must have built his baby up to this fearlessness gradually, each time throwing her slightly higher. By the time I witnessed him throwing her up and catching her, the child had come to love the freedom of flying through the air, knowing she would be caught by her loving father.

This impression of being tossed in the air expresses the deepest reality in human life. God our Father is indeed tossing us in the air. We have only two options: we can either learn to enjoy flying, trusting our Father to catch us and to keep us from harm, or we can be terrified. God says, "Why are you living in fear? Your life is precarious; you are in midair all the time. Remember how often I have already caught you, and learn to enjoy your freedom."

All human life is indeed precarious. Suddenly, we could be dead. Suddenly, we could be stricken with disease. Suddenly, we could be betrayed. Suddenly, our whole world could collapse around us. Therefore we tend to be afraid. People who do not believe there is a loving Father to catch them will live in terror. We must learn to trust that loving Father.

When that baby's father first jiggled her and caught her, she was startled but found the experience exciting and fun. She felt safe; she could trust her father. As he threw her a little higher each time, she remembered that every previous time she was tossed in the air she had been caught, and the more experiences she remembered, the more her trust grew.

We too need to remember how God our Father has saved and rescued us repeatedly in the past. No matter how terrible the events we may have been through, none of them has killed or totally devastated us. We have to *remember* all the times that God has rescued and "caught us" and been a loving Father to us. That is why the Old Testament so often repeats the plea, "Remember." The chief charge made against the people in the Old Testament is, "You forgot. You forgot the God who saved you." When the Israelites were terrified because they had no food, they forgot how they had been trapped at the Red Sea and how God had rescued them. We keep forgetting how often God has caught and saved us in times past.

The parable of the hoarding fool leads directly into two beautiful parables of trust—the ravens and lilies of the field.

Therefore I tell you, do not be anxious about your life *["psychê"]*, what you shall eat, nor about your body, what you shall put on. For life is more than food, and the body

> more than clothing. Consider the ravens: they neither sow
> nor reap, they have neither storehouse nor barn, and yet
> God feeds them. Of how much more value are you than
> the birds!
>
> LUKE 12:22-24

The parable of the ravens echoes both the love commandment and the Lord's Prayer. The same Greek word *"psyché"*
means "life" in "Do not worry about your life," and "soul" in
"Love God with your whole soul." The command to love God
with our whole *"psyché"* tells us to focus our whole self on loving God. If we focus our whole self on loving God, we will not
be able to focus on and worry about ourself.

Yet we often worry about ourselves and our needs. Where
will I get a job or the money I need, or how will I be able to
meet this deadline?

> But if God so clothes the grass which is alive in the field
> today and tomorrow is thrown into the oven, how much
> more will he clothe you, O men of little faith! And do not
> seek what you are to eat and what you are to drink, nor be
> of anxious mind. For all the nations of the world seek these
> things; and your Father knows that you need them.
> Instead, seek his kingdom, and these things shall be yours
> as well.
>
> LUKE 12:28-31

When Jesus tells us to sell our possessions and give alms
(12:33-34), this is an invitation to freedom from anxiety. Such
freedom from anxiety about material security in the future is
another version of the baby up in the air.

Trusting in the Father's Forgiveness—Luke 15

Three parables in Luke 15 help us to follow Jesus with trust in the Father's passionate desire to forgive and his joy in our repentance. The parables respond to a protest by Pharisees and scribes that "This man receives sinners and eats with them." Instead of denying this charge, Jesus' three parables emphasize the tremendous joy God has over a repentant sinner. They make it clear that Jesus is intimate with forgiven sinners, over whose return he rejoices.

The parable of the lost sheep reverses our expectations dramatically. Its "punch line" jars us out of complacency: "Just so, I tell you, there will be more joy in heaven over one sinner who repents than over ninety-nine righteous persons who need no repentance" (Lk 15:7). The parable says that God seeks out even one lost sheep from among the 100 who are not lost. He does not merely write off that lost one as a normal business loss. Everyone is important to God. He would not have created us if he did not long for us to be happy with him forever.

The parable of the lost coin has the same emphasis on God's joy. In this time of inflation, a better example might be one in which a woman turns her house upside down until she finds her lost expensive piece of jewelry. Her joy and relief when she finds it are immense. The angels have this same joy over even one of us sinners who come back to God.

Sometimes after a penitent confesses a particularly embarrassing wrongdoing, or is reconciled again to the church after repenting of an abortion, I feel in myself as confessor God's tremendous surge of love and joy for that person. This emotion of love and joy totally overwhelms any other thoughts or feelings toward the penitent. When penitents hear from me of God's joy, they experience God's joy in their return to him and the assurance that their Father again clasps them in his loving arms.

The parable of the prodigal son offers another startling reversal of expectations. The young son has abused his father's love and has squandered his inheritance. With nothing left, he comes back to his father in remorse.

His father, however, had been watching and longing for his return. "But while he was yet at a distance, his father saw him and had compassion, and ran and embraced him and kissed him" (Lk 15:20). Before the son is able to finish his speech of confession, the father overwhelms him with his love and hospitality. The past is forgiven. The father's joy is overflowing: "Let us eat and make merry; for this my son was dead, and is alive again; he was lost, and is found" (15:23-24).

In order to experience such forgiveness, we prodigals must come back to our Father. We must acknowledge that we have sinned and done wrong. We cannot excuse our wrongdoing and blame someone else, as Adam and Eve did in Genesis 3. Nor can we explain away our sin as psychologically natural, for when we do that we do not return to our Father.

The Father of prodigals stands every day at the crossroads, waiting for our return so that he can show us how he forgives us. Jesus is saying, "The Father has more love and forgiveness to give you than you can fathom. You make God too small, with your cautious expectations of him."

However, the story does not end here. In fact, it could also be called the parable of the unforgiving older son. The older son is angry and jealous of the feasting over his brother. He resents the fact that although he has remained faithful to his father and worked hard for him, his father never provided any feasts in his honor. Yet for his irresponsible brother, the father kills the fatted calf. This is not fair.

Jesus is intentionally overturning our notion of fairness, for it is not God's concept. None of us can measure fairness since none of us can earn heaven as wages for our good work. None of us deserves heaven. All of us have within ourselves the potential for evil of both the prodigal and the jealous older son.

The Christian way is to return to our Father and confess our wrongdoing, to receive his forgiveness when we have sinned. It is to share in God's rejoicing when we or others return to him from our sinful situation. It is to die to our jealousy and to welcome back our sinful brothers and sisters with the same enthusiasm as the Father does. In the Lord's Prayer and these parables, Jesus teaches that our Christian way is one of great peace and joy and trust in our loving Father. As the baby tossed in the air, we can enjoy the excitement and freedom that comes from trusting our Father to catch us.

FOUR

Sharing Jesus' Power for Service

Luke and Acts stress, through both narrative and parable, that disciples who follow Jesus share in his role as servant of the Father's will to save his people. God empowers his servants to accomplish the missions he gives them. That power is intended for the service of God's people, and the teachings of Jesus require corresponding attitudes on the part of his servants.

In Acts 9–10, Servants Imitate Jesus' Miracles in Luke 7

Jesus' favor to the centurion and his raising of the widow's son in Luke 7 resonate in Acts 9–10. In Luke 7:3-4, a centurion sends Jews to intercede with Jesus. They appeal to him, "He [the centurion] is worthy to have you do this for him, for he loves our nation, and he built us our synagogue." In Acts 10:22 a centurion sends servants who ask Peter to come, stating, "Cornelius, a centurion, an upright and God-fearing man, who is well spoken of by the whole Jewish nation, was directed by a holy angel to send for you."

Immediately after the healing of the centurion's servant, Luke 7:11-17 recounts how Jesus raised the widow's son to life. In Acts 9:36-43, immediately before the Cornelius story, Peter raises the widow Dorcas to life. The Nain story begins by mentioning that Jesus' disciples were with him. They observed him as he had compassion on the widow, stopped the bier, and told her son to rise. When the dead son sat up and began to speak, "he [Jesus] gave him to his mother."

In Acts, Peter put the weeping widows outside, knelt down to pray, then commanded the body to rise. When Dorcas sat up, Peter took her by the hand and presented her alive to the widows and the rest of the community. On both occasions, word about the raising spread. Since Luke went out of his way to mention that the disciples were present at the raising of the widow's son, he implies that the disciples learned by observing what Jesus did. In Peter's actions, we see strong parallels to those of Jesus. We also observe in the Gospel narratives the way in which Jesus has pity on people and helps them. Then we are to "go and do likewise."

The disciples in Acts heal as Jesus healed and teach as Jesus taught, but not on their own authority. In the Gospel Jesus acts on his own authority. As disciples of Jesus and servants of God, we receive the authority and power to do what Jesus did, but to do it only in Jesus' name.

Feeding the 5,000: Power to Serve—Luke 9

In Luke 9:1-6, Jesus had sent out the twelve on a training mission; their comprehensive mission would begin only after Pentecost. Jesus prepared them for that mission by drilling them in their message, giving them instructions, and allowing them to make mistakes. When they returned and reported on what they had done (9:10), Jesus showed them how they could improve. Thus, they learned to work on their own, as they would have to do after Jesus was gone.

We too often receive "training missions" when we first experience in a more personal way Jesus and the power of the Holy Spirit. Usually Jesus asks us to do smaller, more ordinary things first. Thus when a group of my students experienced conversion together, they shared their stories with their friends and roommates and brought others to Jesus. They had an evangelistic effect at the university, but not a full-scale mission of evangelization. Meanwhile, they could come for help and supervision to older Christians, learning how to evangelize more effectively. When the disciples report to Jesus or we to more experienced Christians, we can learn from both our successes and mistakes. We can rejoice together and give thanks to God for the way in which he uses us to heal or to bring others to himself.

Jesus often takes his disciples aside for a rest and a chance to let the lessons of their experiences of preaching and healing be assimilated. Christian workers need rest and quiet time. We may be so excited about traveling, preaching, and healing that we do not notice how tired we have become. Jesus wants us to remember our human limitations. No one is made for constant work, nor are any of us so indispensable that we cannot afford to rest from our labors. How often people have felt they could not possibly take time off, yet became sick and were forced to do so.

In Luke 9:10-17, despite Jesus' intention of taking and providing a rest, the people were so hungry for his help that they followed him. When he saw the crowd he had compassion on them, welcomed them, taught them, and cured them. Despite his and his disciples' need for rest, he responded to the needs of others.

This is a model for our Christian behavior. First, we are to care for the needs of our health prudently, by resting and taking time off. Sometimes, however, even when we are being prudent, God allows someone else's need to impinge on our rest. At such times, we can respond as Jesus did with trust that God will give us the requisite strength. He never gives us a task for which he does not also provide the means necessary to accomplish it. The important thing is that we act according to God's will and not our own.

When the twelve express their concern that the crowd needs provisions, Jesus surprises them with the command, "You give them something to eat" (Lk 9:13). When they reply that they have only five loaves and two fish for 5,000 people, Jesus directs them to have the crowd prepare for a meal. This is a critically important lesson for Christian service. When we are sure that Jesus is asking us to do something that seems impossible, and after we have checked to make sure we have not misunderstood him, then, like the twelve, we are to step out in faith and start doing what he asks.

The disciples organize the people in fifties. In language reminiscent of the institution of Eucharist, Luke describes Jesus as looking up to heaven, giving thanks, breaking bread, and giving it to his disciples. Jesus himself does not distribute the bread, but has his disciples pass it out. He delegates; he does not try to handle a crowd of 5,000 by himself.

This example of delegation is very important for Christian leaders today. How many leaders in renewal movements and church organizations have exhausted themselves because they did not know how to delegate, and tried to maintain a personal involvement in everything? Like Jesus, we have to learn to trust others to accomplish the work.

In contrast to the way in which one movie about Jesus presents the feeding of the 5,000, when Jesus blessed and broke the bread and fish, the text gives no indication that suddenly there appeared a huge pile of food. It merely indicates that Jesus gave the pieces to his disciples to set before the crowd. The amount of food never seems sufficient to feed all the hungry and needy; yet as Christians share whatever limited resources they do have, there proves to be enough for everyone.

The disciples had to trust Jesus as they began distributing what must have seemed like a drastically insufficient number of pieces from the five loaves. Only afterward did they retrieve twelve baskets of leftovers. Meanwhile, they simply had to keep breaking off pieces and giving them to the people, trusting that the food would not run out (compare 1 Kings 17:11-16).

If we put ourselves in the place of the disciples, as Luke means us to, we might well feel like fools. How can I feed all these people with this small part of a loaf? Still, I can keep breaking and sharing all that I do have and trust God for the rest. The more we share, the more there is.

The feeding of the 5,000 is a compelling symbol of our work as servants in any Christian ministry. We can begin to feel frustrated about our responsibilities. Where is the time to do all I am supposed to—to write and publish, to teach full time, to act as board and staff member and chaplain for the Institute for Natural Family Planning, to help lead a small committed group of lay Catholics, and to participate in my own Jesuit communal life?

The Lord's answer goes something like this: I am asking you to feed the 5,000 and am giving you five loaves with which to do it. All you have is five loaves of time, energy, and resources. In no way will five loaves be enough. In no way do you now have an adequate amount of time and energy. Nevertheless, just start doing what I ask you to do each day, holding fast to my orders and priorities. Start passing out the loaves piece by piece, proceeding with what you do have and trusting in my resources. If you keep sharing your five loaves you will find that there is enough to feed all.

How liberating this is! We can stop worrying about time. It does mean, however, that we must list our highest priorities and attend to them first. What are the most important priorities? What are the most urgent? When we deal with these priorities first, we do not have to worry about the less important things.

We usually discover that the lesser priorities were not very important. Even though some of them are never completed, their omission does not seem to matter. The key is that our priorities must be God's priorities; we must live and act according to his perfect will. If we are doing what Jesus tells us to do, then we can come forward with peace and trust having only five loaves to feed 5,000 people. We are merely his servants, following his instructions. It is our Lord's responsibility to make sure there is enough for all.

Further Lessons on Being Servants—Luke 12

Luke's Gospel illustrates how disciples are servants of God. Several parables about servants in his Gospel reveal a great deal about what it means to be a servant.

First, since we are servants, we are not the person in charge.

We are only the hired help. We neither set policy nor take responsibility for the success of the company. We can contribute to the company's success by doing our own task well and responsibly, but ultimately we will get our wages from God whether the company has an overall profit or loss. The "buck does not stop" with us but with Jesus.

If we sense that we are anxious about what we are doing as God's servants, we need to ask what might be causing this anxiety. When tempted to become anxious about something, we can best turn our anxiety into a prayer. If I am worried about meeting a deadline, I ask God to help me meet it. If I am anxious about what to say to someone with whom I strongly disagree, I ask God for the right words and the peace in which to say them.

This lesson proved a major blessing during my summer in Nigeria. I was to help a Jesuit friend give some retreats to religious sisters and some Bible conferences to lay leaders of charismatic prayer groups. This mission was part of my final training as a Jesuit. We had an hour's trip to our next retreat, and it was about an hour and a half before dark. Because it was very dangerous to travel at night in this part of the country, we wanted to reach our destination quickly. Yet we had forgotten to get gasoline for the car. It took some time before we found an open gas station, and when we did find one it had a long line of cars. At the pump, cars kept cutting into the line. We had no assurance, even if we waited patiently in line, that we would get to the pump before it ran out of gas.

The temptation to worry was enormous, but God helped me to pray instead. I kept praying as people tried to cut in ahead of us. My prayer that we could get gas and arrive at the locality of our next retreat before dark may have been a somewhat anxious one, but it was still prayer and not merely worry! Despite the difficulty, we got our gas and reached our destination just at nightfall.

When we refuse to worry and pray instead, God lifts our cares from our shoulders. We are asking the Master to give us, his workers, tools that we need to do his task. "Lord, if you want me to advise this troubled pregnant teenager, you have to give me the right words." "If you want me to form committed relationships with these brothers in my religious community, please show me how and give me the time and patience and selfless love to do it." Prayer hands over the problem to God for him to solve. We in turn can be at peace, no matter how serious the problems that face us.

Servants live their lives according to the schedules of others. Often the urgent need of another person interrupts what they are doing. Such disruptions can be a source of frustration and anxiety, if we do not turn them over to God. Jesus himself expected to rest but the needs of the 5,000 intruded into his rest. The need of the wounded stranger interrupted the plans of the Good Samaritan. One of the greatest trials of parents is constant interruption by small children.

As servants, we cannot be concerned with what other people think of us as long as we know we are doing what our Master wants. We cannot be too attached to any particular role or task. The servant whom the Lord can shift to any work that needs doing is considerably more useful to him than one who can or will do only one particular task.

The first parable, in Luke 12:35-48, challenges us to be ready as God's servants. Servants conform their schedules to the wishes of their Master; they do not ask their Master to adjust to theirs. Servants stay up all night in readiness for their Master's return; they do not make him wait until they wake up to come down to open the door. Blessed are those servants who are ready at any watch of the night. "You also must be ready; for the Son of Man is coming at an hour you do not expect" (12:40).

We do not know when Christ will return. He could come soon or he could delay his return further. In several sayings, Jesus tells us that his return will be without warning, so that we must always be ready. Nor are we to become preoccupied with signs of his coming.

The following parable in Luke 12:41-48 indicates that there are various classes of servants. Peter's question, "Lord, are you telling this parable for us or for all?" implies this. Jesus' new parable explicitly mentions a steward, a servant whom the master sets over all the other servants of the household. Stewards or managers are also servants, but they have delegated authority from their master over other servants.

The pope calls himself "the servant of the servants of God." He is a fellow human servant whom God has appointed manager over the rest of us. His authority over us is a form of service that facilitates the functioning of the whole church. His authority is not for the sake of power or domination.

The secular world clothes authority with many symbols of power to entice successful people to leave lucrative jobs for political positions. Marks of power may be a necessary evil in the secular world, but they ought not to be the Christian approach to positions of authority in the church. The Gospels make abundantly clear that church authority is exclusively for service, not for power. The model of authority based on power entirely misses the point that stewards serve the church by providing the authority necessary for unity.

Luke 12:47-48 continues Jesus' sobering warnings to church leaders. Although Jesus usually talks of mercy for sinners, certain kinds of sin merit extremely harsh punishments. Abuse of authority in the church is high on this list. Jesus says he will remove from authority such abusive managers. Similarly, false teachers who, like wolves in sheep's clothing, cause one of his little ones to sin would be better off thrown into the sea with a millstone around their neck (Lk 17:1-2). Out of his concern for all the sheep of his flock, Jesus promises severe punishment for abuses of the leadership role.

These are very sobering pictures of what it means to be a steward or manager in Christ's church. If we are placed in authority, we are not to expect recognition, honor, power, or material gains from our service. We are here to perform a task. The Christian community cannot function in unity without an authority. A body without a head has no life. Two-headed bodies are not particularly successful either.

There can be only one authority in a community, although more than one person may share in it. If the relatively recent notion of a "double magisterium" is interpreted as two independent sets of teaching authorities, with theologians claiming authority equal or parallel to that of pope and bishops, this notion cannot but undermine the church's unity. Experience of such a "double magisterium" in the past three decades has amply demonstrated the confusion and disunity that results.

Many theologians are sincerely committed to serving the church through intellectual honesty and sound methods of reasoning. When their research results in conclusions at odds with the current official teaching of the pope and bishops, the church must discern whether these "new" conclusions represent an appropriate understanding of the mysteries of revelation for a new situation, or whether they are a distortion of the Good News. The pope and bishops normally do this in consultation with theologians and other faithful. In this manner the teachings of theologians can legitimately influence the official teaching of pope and bishops.

But because the pope with the bishops in union with him are the sole official teaching authority within the church, they alone are ultimately responsible and authorized to judge whether a theologian's teaching is acceptable for the Catholic Church. Despite the important contribution theologians make to the church's understanding of revelation, they cannot be a second magisterium in competition with the authority of pope and bishops. When theologians practice a "theology of dissent" that persists in teaching something explicitly rejected by the highest teaching authority within the church, they confuse the ordinary faithful. Some thirty years of dissent has quite thoroughly undermined the church's catechesis of the last two generations of American Catholics, as my experience both as university professor and as priest amply attests.

The Scriptures leave no doubt that there is only one official teaching authority in the church. That is the apostolic authority of Peter and the apostles. In the Catholic Church today, that apostolic authority resides exclusively in the pope and the bishops in union with him.

The church has never ordained or officially commissioned professional theologians as such to be church authorities, even though many theologians have been ordained bishops and in that way been incorporated into the official magisterium. Thus as a Catholic professional theologian who am not myself a bishop, I submit my insights to acceptance or rejection by official church teachers, the pope and the bishops in union with him.

The Parable of the Worldly-wise Steward—Luke 16:1-15

This unsettling parable raises several questions. Even though the master has dismissed the steward for wasting the master's goods, he apparently commends the steward for his dishonest dealings with the master's debtors. Jesus was here commending not dishonesty but the shrewdness with which the steward provided for his needs. "For the sons of this world are more shrewd in dealing with their own generation than the sons of light" (16:8).

Jesus appeals to us his followers, "Why are you not as resourceful and hard-working for God as worldly people are for material goods and secular influence? Why do you not search and discover all available possibilities as do people of the world? Why do people who work for corporations slave with so much greater initiative and at so much higher cost to their personal lives than my own followers do for God's work?"

Luke 16:10-13 emphasizes that as servants of God we are stewards who administer the resources of our master according to his instructions. God gives us our lives, bodies, talents, time, and money as resources to use in his service. They are not our own to do with as we please. We are not to abuse our bodies with overwork, overeating, drunkenness, sexual license, lack of exercise, or too much or too little sleep. We are only stewards of everything we have. If we are faithful in using what God gives us, as he intended, he will give us great treasures in heaven.

Luke 16:13 makes a very important point about our status as God's servants. "No servant can serve two masters; for either he will hate the one and love the other, or he will be devoted to the one and despise the other. You cannot serve God and mammon." God will not share our loyalty and service with other masters. "You shall love the Lord your God with all your heart, and with all your soul, and with all your strength, and with all your mind" (Lk 10:27).

If we have divided loyalties, other people and Satan can manipulate us. If we are pulled in opposite directions, unable to choose between God and wealth, power, security, success, fame, or acceptance by others, we furnish others means by which to control us. Others can coerce us to acquiesce in injustice if we are too afraid of losing our jobs. Others can manipulate us into sin if we depend too much on their acceptance. We cannot serve God and anything or anyone else.

Luke tempers the joy and enthusiasm for which he is especially noted with a sobering call to become mature servants. Immature people can do much damage to God's cause or harm those whom they are trying to help. The Lord calls us into ever-increasing maturity as his servants. God may love us as we are, but he certainly expects us to continue to grow. We love our children as they are, but we do not allow them to continue to act like children when they get older. One of the harshest things we can say to an adult is to "stop acting like a baby."

The parable in Luke 17:7-10 also brings us up short. Jesus is describing how people actually treat servants in secular life, not giving an idealistic picture of how to treat our own servants. A secular manager does not invite the servant who has been working in the fields all day to come and dine with him. Nor is he obliged to thank his servant for what he has already paid him to do.

Servants cannot demand gratitude. The point of the parable is in the last line: "So you also, when you have done all that is commanded you, say, 'We are unworthy servants; we have only done what was our duty'" (17:10). We do not serve in order to find our self-worth or to be complimented.

Finally, Luke 19:11-27 speaks of the resources God gives all of us as talents to use in his service. To some he gives more, to others less. But he praises whoever does the best he can with what he has. The only servant God condemns is the one who hides his talent out of fear, so that he does not even earn interest on the money entrusted to him. Fear cripples service. This parable maintains that fear is no excuse for not using our talents. We must directly confront whatever we fear, trusting that God is with us.

In summary, God calls us to be his servants as Jesus was his servant. God wants us to provide for his people's needs with the power he gives us. God wants us to trust him for the results of our service. He warns us not to take advantage of the fellow servants he entrusts to our care. He reminds us that we are only stewards of our lives and must use them according to his design. He asks undivided loyalty from us, and a maturity that does not always seek praise or affirmation for our work. He tells us to confront our fears directly and not let them keep us from his work. All these parables call us to the kind of selfless service of God's people that Jesus exemplifies.

FIVE

The Cost of Salvation to Jesus and the Disciples

Sometime after the initial enthusiasm of conversion or after the fervent realization that God loves us, we face a major turning point in our walk with Jesus. A baby receives without giving but an adult must learn to give as well as to receive. In our Christian life, we must grow beyond the stage of merely receiving God's love and forgiveness to that of giving to others what we received. At this turning point, we begin to realize what it cost Jesus to save us and what it costs us to follow in his footsteps.

This chapter will focus on three parts of Luke's Gospel that emphasize this cost. Luke 9:18-27 is a turning point for the disciples as they learn the cost of discipleship. Three sets of sayings (in Lk 12:1-11, 14:25-35, and 18:18-30) bring out further aspects of the cost of following Jesus. Finally, Jesus gives his farewell instructions to his disciples at the Last Supper (Lk 22:14-38).

A New Level of Discipleship—Luke 9:18-27

Previous accounts of Jesus' inviting disciples, his exchange with evil spirits and deliverance of those possessed by them, his forgiveness of sins, and his feeding of the 5,000 prepare Luke's readers for this turning point in the disciples' relationship to Jesus. Up to this point, Jesus has not talked openly about who he is. He has even tried to prevent people and evil spirits from talking too much about his miracles or his identity. In Jesus' prayer, the Father indicates to him that now is the time to reveal himself. Before this, his disciples had not been ready; even now, they will misunderstand what being Messiah implies, both for Jesus and for them.

One of the great temptations in following Jesus is to try to accelerate God's timetable. We usually forget how long it took us to come to any new awareness, and we become impatient with others who have not attained the same insight. For a number of years, for example, I agreed with the commonly accepted explanation of evil spirits as merely personifications of evil. Then I began reading trustworthy accounts and hearing from friends who had freed persons suffering from severe apparently psychological oppression by commanding personal evil spirits to leave these people. I found the notion and reality of exorcism very hard to accept, but I knew that the people who reported these events were not crazy, lying, nor ignorant.

Subsequently I myself began having pastoral experiences of problems that did not seem explicable except through the machinations of personal evil spirits. When, despite my misgivings, I commanded spirits to leave in Jesus' name, I saw dramatic and instant improvement in those suffering. In addition, at least at times I pronounced these commands silently so that the afflicted person could not even hear me. These silent commands too resulted in immediate and dramatic improvement in the victim's condition. I became convinced that personal evil spirits are real. I no longer try to explain away the exorcisms in Scripture and church history.

After changing my own opinion so laboriously and with so many struggles, I had to remind myself how long it had taken me to attain my new awareness. I could not give in to impatience with others who had not had this experience, and who, not unreasonably, doubted as I myself had done for so long. Like Jesus, I had to let the Father show me when to speak about some controversial matter and when to wait until others were more ready to listen to what I held to be true.

When Jesus asked his disciples, "Who do the people say that I am?" (Lk 9:18), they gave him a variety of answers, all of which identified Jesus with prophetic figures. Neither the question nor the answers demanded any personal commitment on the disciples' part. At that point Jesus challenged them personally: "But who do you say that I am?" (9:20). The disciples could no longer hide behind the opinions of other people. They had to say what they believed.

It is so easy to hide behind the opinions of others. For a scholar and teacher, it is very tempting simply to list the opinions of other scholars and, especially in emotionally charged controversies, to hide one's own view behind reports about what others hold. However, we cannot be followers of Jesus without taking a personal stand. No matter what we say, some people will not like our statement. For example, it is not fashionable in some theological circles to confess that Jesus is the Second Person of the Trinity become incarnate as a fully human person—true God and true man.

Jesus, however, asks each of us to take our stand. I am not ashamed to confess to Jesus the following beliefs that I hold. I call you my Lord and my God. I worship you as God with the Father and the Holy Spirit. I worship you both as at the Father's right hand in heaven and as present in a special sacramental way in the Eucharist. I worship and adore you at both the Eucharistic liturgy and when I visit you reserved in the Blessed Sacrament in churches. I recognize you present when two or more are gathered in your name.

In your name I pray for physical, spiritual, and psychological healing. In your name I take authority over evil spirits. In your name I forgive people's sins in the Sacrament of Reconciliation. I try to imitate you as fully human, and I adore you as divine. I feel an intimate kinship with you because you are human as I myself am; I feel an awe before you as my God.

If Jesus is not all this, then many generations of Christians, including myself, are idolaters and blasphemers, worshipping as divine what is merely human. A standard theological dictum is *"Lex orandi lex credendi."* That is, the way in which the church prays and worships leads to the statements in creeds of what the church believes.

In the liturgy, Christians constantly pray to Jesus as God as well as man. Over my entire lifetime, my personal religious experience has both been based on and confirmed my belief that Jesus is God as well as man. Similarly, Christians through the centuries have worshipped Jesus as God. Theologians who nevertheless argue against the divinity of Jesus ignore, deny, or explain away all this religious experience and the witness of Scripture for the sake of their theories. Their positions ought not remain without challenge.

Peter's answer to Jesus in Luke 9:20 is not as expansive as my own answer above. Luke emphasizes the humanity of Jesus, because he considers it important to stress continuity between the church and its Old Testament roots and the promises it fulfills. Therefore Peter's answer as spokesman for the disciples is "You are God's Messiah," the one God promised in Old Testament prophecy.

In response, Jesus charges the disciples to tell this to no one and predicts his passion and death. Before Jesus' crucifixion, the belief that he was the Messiah was too apt to be misunderstood in a political sense (Lk 23:2). On the other hand, only when we realize who Jesus really is, our Messiah, the Savior who will take care of us, are we ready for the message of the cross.

This dialogue between Jesus and Peter presents a model that has critical importance for Christian life. In experiences of conversion, we first allow Jesus to rescue us from our sins and alienation from God, and we break off our futile attempts to earn our own reconciliation with God. We accept God's forgiveness and believe that he loves us. We accept whatever healing Jesus wants to give us. As we mature in our Christian living, we become more able to consider what our forgiveness and reconciliation cost Jesus.

Christ's obedience was required to make up for our disobedience, in order that alienated humanity might be reconciled with God. The new Adam obeys where the old Adam disobeyed. Jesus reconciles us with God through his self-emptying servanthood, which atones for the self-seeking of humanity (cf. Phil 2:5-11).

It cost even God to save us from condemnation. In the Old Testament, God frequently rescued the Jews, but it apparently cost God nothing to destroy the pursuers of the Israelites in the Red Sea, or to provide manna in the desert. In contrast, the forgiveness of our sins cost the Father his only Son. It cost the incarnate Son rejection, torture, and death.

We need only to look at the crucifixion to resist a temptation, very widespread today, to explain away sin. Anything that could cost God the death of his only Son can only be utterly evil, repulsive, and destructive. Even some preachers and religious educators tend to reduce sin to a psychological problem: "Johnny could not help what he did because his parents did not love him enough." We tend to rationalize self-seeking and self-indulgent sins like greed, gossip, jealousy, lust, anger, and ambition. The cross gives our rationalizations the lie.

Christ says to all of us: "If any man would come after me, let him deny himself and take up his cross daily and follow me. For whoever would save his life will lose it; and whoever loses his life for my sake, he will save it. For what does it profit a man if he gains the whole world and loses or forfeits himself?" (Lk 9:23-25).

We must abandon our attempts to justify and excuse ourselves. Instead, we need to be willing to lose ourselves for Christ's sake and to allow him to reconcile us to his Father and to provide for our needs. This instruction to become mature disciples strikes at the very heart of our deepest fears, for those who try to rescue themselves often become afraid.

If we are crossing the street and notice a car bearing down on us, fear removes us from its path without our having to think about it. Fear can save our lives. However, fear can also make us self-seeking. Jesus tells us that the greatest love is to give up one's life for one's friends. Such great love casts out self-seeking fear.

If we keep striving to save ourselves and our own lives we will probably be too preoccupied with anxiety to open ourselves up to receive Jesus' saving love or to share our lives with others. Our lives will remain enclosed within a wall of fear. Such anxiety in our lives can also lead us to strike out at others or to flee from them.

Jesus invites us to entrust our well-being to him. We do not need to travel solo through life fending off disasters and scraping for our subsistence. That is the animal life of the jungle. Such an existence is lonely, self-preoccupied, and ridden with fear. Instead of the life of fear, fight, and flight, Jesus offers us a life of trust in him and in others, whom we learn to see not as competitors fighting over the world's limited supplies but as brothers and sisters of the heavenly Father who feeds us all.

St. Paul refers to a similar situation when he contrasts life lived according to the flesh with that lived according to the Spirit (Gal 5:13-26). By "flesh," Paul means human character traits devoted to self-preservation on one's own without God's help. The flesh produces "immorality, impurity, licentiousness" as ways in which to escape the loneliness and boredom of self-centered living. It produces "idolatry and sorcery" as ways in which to control one's environment and provide for one's needs. "Enmity, strife, jealousy, anger, selfishness, dissension, party spirit, and envy" result from competing for limited goods, each person for himself or herself. "Drunkenness, carousing, and the like" become escapes from the anxiety of such an isolated jungle existence (Gal 5:19-21).

"Those who do such things [the works of the flesh] shall not inherit the kingdom of God" (Gal 5:21). Not only do we need to face this fact ourselves, we must also affirm it clearly to those for whom we are responsible—our children, students, parishioners, and all under our authority or influence.

If we entrust our lives to Jesus and walk according to the guidance of his Spirit, we will find a happiness that jungle living cannot provide. "But the fruit of the Spirit is love, joy, peace, patience, kindness, goodness, faithfulness, gentleness, self-control" (Gal 5:22-23). These are the signs of the life we find when we give up trying to preserve our own interests.

Peace replaces fear and anxiety. Love and joy replace lonely striving for ourselves and for our own needs. Kindness and the rest of these fruits are marks of shared life in a Christian community. For "those who belong to Christ Jesus have crucified the flesh with its passions and desires" (Gal 5:24).

Jesus' sayings about finding and losing our lives and selves directly contradict the "selfism" that dominates our culture. Selfism makes oneself the center of the universe. "I" am the touchstone of everything. Bookstores have whole sections full of books that promote self-fulfillment and self-actualization.

The crass self-promotion of various contemporary books and songs has its recent ancestry in such titles from the 1960s and 1970s as *Looking Out for Number One* and *Winning Through Intimidation*. For decades, our culture has been blatantly encouraging us to climb over others to get ahead ourselves, to use others as sexual objects, to ruin our competitors in business to enrich ourselves. Conventional wisdom crassly advises abandoning a marriage or any other commitment if it is not "actualizing our potential."

Following Jesus requires a constant battle against the selfism that is so ingrained in us and in our culture.

Shows and advertisements constantly tempt us to buy far more than we need. They encourage us to put our own careers before any relationships and to emphasize security for the future. They urge us to pamper ourselves, to be quite self-conscious about how we look or smell, to prove our sexual prowess by engaging in promiscuous relationships, etc. Jesus challenges us, "If any man would come after me, let him deny himself and take up his cross daily and follow me" (Lk 9:23). Rather than promoting ourselves, we are to forget ourselves and trust in God.

In effect, Jesus is asking us to die to ourselves in order to unite with him. He is asking us to form one interdependent "we" with him, in place of many independent "I's." That is why Ephesians calls marriage a symbol of the union between Christ and his church. The union of two in one flesh in marriage is a sign of the union the church should have with Christ.

When spouses insist on their own independence, on the priority of career over the commitments of marriage, on contracts delineating each partner's tasks and roles, on separate bank accounts, etc., these spouses' relationship begins to look more like a preparation for future divorce or even like the agreement between two single roommates than like a Christian marriage. Unfortunately, the prevalence of cohabitation before marriage often perpetuates behavior more appropriate to singles sharing an apartment than to spouses.

The only way in which two can become one is for both to let go of their independence and become interdependent. We too will be unable to live genuine communal lives if we constantly insist on our own rights, our own needs, and our own priorities. Nor can we have community if we refuse to trust one another.

Suffering for One's Faith in Christ—Luke 12:1-12

In three sayings, Jesus develops the implications of saving or losing one's life and applies this pattern to our lives.

Luke 12:1-3 warns us against hypocrisy. What we whisper in the dark will become public. As disciples of Jesus, we are to live in such a way that every aspect of our lives remains "in the light." We must die to a certain kind of "private life." If we are keeping any habitual activity or any relationship in the dark, unwilling that others should learn of it, something about that activity or relationship is evidently wrong.

"Living in the light" is the best safeguard against falling away from Christ into irreversible sinful situations. If married people let their spouses know about every relationship they have, they are not likely to fall into adulterous affairs. If priests and celibate religious are accountable to others for every relationship they have, they will experience an effective protection against becoming disloyal to their vows.

Luke 12:4-7 exhorts us to die to our fears of those who could kill us. Jesus assures us we need not fear even physical death or earthly persecution, but ought rather fear anyone who could cause us to lose our eternal life with God. As we give up our fears of losing our lives, we find new freedom and peace based on trust in God, who protects us.

Luke 12:8-12 applies this principle explicitly to confessing Christ in the face of persecution. Jesus expects his disciples to confess him before men and warns us against denying him. If we try to save our lives by denying Christ, we will lose eternal life with him. If, however, we lose our lives, jobs, or reputations by confessing Christ, we will find eternal life with him. He will stand by us at the Judgment.

Nevertheless, "Every one who speaks a word against the Son of Man will be forgiven; but he who blasphemes against the Holy Spirit will not be forgiven" (Lk 12:10). What does this shocking statement mean? Jesus forgave Peter, who denied him. He forgave those who blasphemed him while he was hanging on the cross. However, Acts makes clear that it is worse to reject Jesus today, after his resurrection and after Pentecost, than during his lifetime. Acts plainly demonstrates that the Holy Spirit sent by the glorified Jesus provided unambiguous signs of Jesus' lordship, which were unavailable to many during his lifetime.

Those who rejected Jesus on the cross but later accepted his lordship could yet be reconciled to God, but those who refuse conversion after the manifest sign of Pentecost are "blaspheming against the Holy Spirit" (cf. Lk 12:10). One should not label as blasphemy against the Spirit the discomfort that numerous Catholics experience at unfamiliar manifestations of the Holy Spirit such as speaking in tongues or other phenomena of Pentecostalism or charismatic renewal. Blasphemy against the Holy Spirit is far more serious. It entails a refusal to accept God's forgiveness and love. How can even God forgive the sin of refusing to accept forgiveness?

Why do people refuse to accept God's forgiveness? Often they fear losing control over their own lives. To accept forgiveness means to admit we were wrong and to resolve to change our behavior. We cannot accept Jesus as Savior without also permitting him to be Lord over our whole lives.

The Holy Spirit's revelation at Pentecost took away the excuse of ignorance that many of Jesus' contemporaries had. We humans are able to refuse to believe even what we see with our own eyes. Such ignorance is willful blindness and is culpable; it is also very common today.

When couples want a child, they call it their baby as soon as they discover the pregnancy. When they do not want the next child, they call it a fetus. Signs warn pregnant women that smoking or drinking is dangerous to babies in the womb. However, advertisements and arguments for abortion never use the expression "baby in the womb."

God leaves us free to reject even the evidence we see, and he respects the choices we make with our free will. Whereas animals have no choice but to serve God according to their instincts, humans are free to accept or reject his love and to believe or disbelieve in God. If we choose to reject God, he respects our choice for all eternity, and that is what we mean by hell.[1]

During our lifetimes, we can always change. Now is always the acceptable time for repenting, changing our minds, and accepting his love. Death seals the direction we have chosen in life. That is why Scripture is so urgent that we not delay returning to God. We do not know how much time we have left to do so.

The church has always refused to declare that everyone will be saved. That would imply that God forces the love of those who reject him. That would also trivialize our human choices during this life. God has an awesome respect for human choice, and we too must take our choices and their consequences seriously.

Counting the Cost of Discipleship—Luke 14:25-35

In this section, Jesus almost gives the impression of wanting to discourage large crowds from accompanying him. His sayings appear intense, even harsh. Jesus seems to be saying that he would rather have resolute commitment in a few dedicated disciples than a mass of mediocre followers.

> If any one comes to me and does not hate his own father and mother and wife and children and brothers and sisters, yes, and even his own life, he cannot be my disciple. Whoever does not bear his own cross and come after me, cannot be my disciple.
>
> LUKE 14:26-27

Many have misunderstood this hard saying. The problematic word is "hate." Hate and love are opposites, and in Scripture, neither term is associated primarily with feelings but rather with willed choices. What I love is what I choose; what I hate is what I reject. If we find ourselves compelled to make a choice between God and our family, we must choose God. This choice is not as common today as it was in the early church, when conversion to Christianity often brought rejection by one's family.

Even today, it remains enormously traumatic for a Jewish or Muslim family if one of its members converts to Christianity. Some families disinherit and cut off converted members. Familial rejection was even more common in the first century, among not only Jewish but also pagan families. Christianity appeared to many as one of the numerous strange cults in the Roman Empire. In that age or this, Jesus' saying speaks strongly to disinherited Christians, who had to choose Christ over their families.

Rejection by families was another reason why Christian community became so essential in the early church. People who lose their blood families need another family. Early Christian communities tried to provide such familial support, taking care of orphans, widows, and those in need. Some Christians today experience a similar rejection from their own secularized families. They too need a supportive environment in which to live the radical values of Christianity.

The two parables in Luke 14:28-33 underscore our need to look at the cost of being a close follower of Christ. Jesus does not want us to blunder into a commitment without knowing what it costs. He does not want people to start following him and then walk out on him.

The first parable discusses building a tower without first having determined what financing is necessary to complete it. Leaving an unfinished foundation is more shameful than having no building at all. The second parable asks whether a king with 10,000 soldiers dares do battle against one with 20,000. If he does not weigh these odds before he acts, he could meet a disastrous defeat. Jesus does not want his followers to have any illusions. He wants us to know to what we are saying yes.

Luke has been leading up to a displeasing conclusion: "So therefore, whoever of you does not renounce all that he has cannot be my disciple" (Lk 14:33). We can follow Jesus only if we are willing to give up *everything*, and cling to nothing. If we try to maintain control of anything at all, we will not be single-hearted but torn between two masters.

The world, the flesh, and the devil will then possess means by which to turn us away from Jesus. Once we surrender everything, we will realize that God cannot be outdone in generosity, as he returns to us a hundredfold compared to what we gave to him. However, his gifts are not our personal possessions, but something we hold in trust. We are God's stewards for our families, our relationships, our material possessions, our health and time. These points become especially clear in Jesus' encounter with the rich ruler.

Renouncing Possessions and Receiving God's Reward—Luke 18:18-30

Jesus' answer to the rich man makes it plain that to follow him will have an effect on our pocketbooks. The monetary cost of discipleship is a significant theme throughout Luke and Acts. If we want to know where our heart really is, we should look at how we actually spend our money and time. A conversion or change of heart will result in a change of how we spend money and time.

As I watch many of my close friends, I see their ever deepening conversion of heart result eventually in their hearing God ask them personally to do what Scripture asks, to tithe or give back to him one tenth of their income (before taxes). For example, if their salary is $50,000 a year, $5,000 of that is set aside for God's work, and they consider only the $45,000 before taxes as available for their budget. As they enter more deeply into the trust needed to tithe, they discover that God more than amply provides for their own needs with the other 90 percent.

Conversion in our use of money affects the remaining 90 percent of our income as well. It means helping from our own resources people who need help. It can sometimes mean even communal sharing of goods, as in religious orders (compare Acts 4:32-35). We love God with our money through tithing and we love our neighbor as ourselves when we share and give alms.

When the rich ruler asks, "What shall I do to inherit eternal life" he expects Jesus' initial response, which was to obey the commandments. Without hesitation, he can claim that he has not committed adultery, murdered, stolen, nor borne false witness, and that he has honored his parents. Jesus' counter-response, however, deflates him: "One thing you still lack. Sell all that you have and distribute to the poor, and you will have treasure in heaven; and come, follow me" (Lk 18:22). He had not expected Jesus to ask him to give up his riches.

Jesus' next statement not only shocked the original listeners, but it continues to disturb Christians through the centuries: "How hard it is for those who have riches to enter the kingdom of God! For it is easier for a camel to go through the eye of a

needle than for a rich man to enter the kingdom of God....
[Then who can be saved?] ... What is impossible with men is
possible with God" (Lk 18:24-27).

How often have we been in air-conditioned churches where
the preacher is forced to say something about this passage!
Having rummaged around in the commentaries, he resorts to
the theory about a gate in Jerusalem called the Eye of the
Needle, which was so low that a camel had to hunch down to
get through. However, the camel could not pass through if it
was carrying a sizable load. Unfortunately for such explanations,
scholars today deny such a theory: Jesus meant the eye of an
actual needle. Even if thread were a lot thicker in those days,
even if the needle were big enough to thread a rope, there were
not many camels small enough to get through the eye of that
needle!

How are we to interpret and apply in our lives such hard sayings? The strictly literal sense does not seem applicable, for this
maxim could imply that all rich people will find themselves in
hell. Nevertheless, Jesus does intend these statements to be
taken quite seriously. He intends them to shock us out of our
complacency and to force us to ask what they could mean for
our lives. Even if these texts are too extreme to be taken literally,
they clearly indicate the direction in which Jesus wants our solution to go.

Scholars call such sayings a "focal instance." These sayings
offer an extreme example that severely challenges our ordinary
values. Proverbs about camels going through eyes of needles or
about gouging out one's eye shock us. They get us to question
values that we have taken for granted. They compel us to ask, as
the first listeners did, how we can nevertheless be saved. They
leave the application free, but the direction is quite clear.

Peter's answer takes the saying at its face value. "Lo, we have left our homes and followed you" (Lk 18:28). The disciples traveling with Jesus have even literally done what Jesus asked. Jesus replies that God's generosity will dwarf even theirs. Those who have left house, wife, brothers, parents, or children for the kingdom of God will receive many times more in this age, and eternal life in the next.

If we have given up our family, we will discover assistance within the church. If we have left behind our own money and resources, God and the church community can take care of all our needs. Leaving everything to follow Christ brings us back to the lilies of the field and to losing our lives in order to save them. These sayings challenge us to trust in the Father, that he will provide for us a new family in the form of communal life and support within the church.

SIX

Jesus' Way Leads to Passion and to Victory

The Bible has a number of farewell scenes, in which some-one says goodbye to sons or disciples immediately before death. These farewell addresses emphasize aspects of the dying person's life or teachings that are particularly important for future generations. They often contain predictions about bless-ings or problems for later generations. Luke refocuses his account of the Last Supper to emphasize Jesus' farewell to his twelve apostles (Lk 22:14, 29-30).

Jesus' Farewell—Luke 22:14-38

Jesus begins his farewell by telling his disciples how he longed to eat this Passover with them before his suffering. He gives them the farewell gift of the Eucharist. We remember Jesus through the Eucharist, which, at the Last Supper, foreshadowed Jesus' self-giving on the cross and which, now, makes that self-giving present to us. This memento of his death is so sacred, that we must be wary of the movement over the last couple decades toward trivializing the Eucharist into predominantly a fellowship meal, with no reference to Christ's sacrifice for us.

During the farewell conversation between Jesus and his apos-tles, the Lord recalls those things he most wants them to remember. First, he prepares them for the shock that one of them will betray him to his death. Then he counters a dispute among them over who should be regarded as the greatest, by giving an emphatic teaching about the true meaning of Christian authority.

> The kings of the Gentiles exercise lordship over them and those in authority over them are called benefactors. But not so with you; rather let the greatest among you become as the youngest, and the leader as one who serves.... But I am among you as one who serves.
>
> Luke 22:25-27

At this most solemn moment of Jesus' life, he reminds us that Christian authority is a way in which to serve one another.

Jesus promises the twelve that one day, after their trials, they will judge the restored twelve tribes of Israel. He especially strengthens Peter so that he may recover from his denials and strengthen his brothers. He warns the disciples to be ready for much more suffering than they have encountered while he was training them. Similarly, Jesus does not spare us from trials and failures, but prepares us for them, even using them to strengthen us so that we can in turn lead and help others. He recalls our hope of resurrection after the death we must all endure.

Jesus' Struggle to Accept His Death—Luke 22:39-46

Christians commonly refer to this passage as the "Agony in the Garden." The Greek word *"agon"* also means "struggle," like a wrestling match, and that is the way in which Luke describes this event. Luke depicts Jesus wrestling with an unnamed adversary concerning his impending passion. Since Luke does not specify with whom Jesus is wrestling, we might understand the contender to be God, as Jacob wrestled with the Lord under the guise of an angel in the Old Testament. Or else the combatant could be Satan in his last and greatest attempt to tempt Jesus.

Jesus begins by warning his disciples to pray with him: "Pray that you may not enter into temptation" (Lk 22:40). The Greek also means, "Pray that you may not succumb to the test." Often we will face things that cause fear and anxiety in us. Jesus does not free us from temptation or from facing fearful events, but he does give us an approach for overcoming our fear.

If I personally find myself anxious, the Lord is challenging me to pray. As I do pray, I usually find peace. During the years since I first wrote this, I have learned from recurring experience that the primary key to peace is to surrender and abandon myself and my fear and concern to God, as Jesus did at the climax of his struggle in the garden. I can then face whatever caused the anxiety with all my powers of concentration, and not be hindered by fear.

As usual, Jesus not only instructs his disciples to pray, but he gives them his personal example as a model of how to follow his instructions. He withdrew about a stone's throw, so his disciples could see him praying as he was speaking freely to his Father. His prayer in this testing strongly echoes the Lord's Prayer: In Luke's gospel, both begin with "Father." Jesus asks that his Father remove the passion from his path. Like us, he experienced fear. Like us, he was tempted. However, unlike us, he always overcame fear and temptation, remaining faithful to his Father's will.

In his fear, Jesus turns to God as his Father. His example

shows us that when we are afraid, we are not to approach God as Lord and master, nor as judge. As children run to their father when they are afraid, Jesus teaches us to run to our Father in our fears, with the confidence and intimacy of children. Nor do children censor their requests to their parents. If they want a candy bar, they simply ask for it. They do not first ask themselves whether it is good for their teeth! In the same way, we need not censor our requests to God. Jesus demonstrated the freedom to ask his Father that the passion might pass him by if possible.

Little children also realize that they will not always get what they ask for. When they ask for a candy bar, they are aware that their mother might respond in several ways. She might give them one, or she might say that it is too close to supper. She might offer them an apple instead. Similarly, with God we are simply to ask for what we want and then listen for God's response.

When we are sick, we spontaneously ask for healing. God may heal us, either immediately, or gradually, or at a time when we are more ready to adjust to the change of the healing. We may find our ultimate healing in death and in the heavenly peace that follows. In answer to our prayer God may not give us physical healing but something that we need even more, such as interior peace, freedom from anger, or a surrender to his providence when our sickness forces us to admit we are helpless before God.

When Jesus asked to be spared the rejection and torture of the cross, Luke shows us that it was not as easy for him to accept the Father's answer as the words of his prayer might imply: "And being in an agony he prayed more earnestly; and his sweat became like drops of blood falling down upon the ground"

(22:44). It took a long and agonized prayer before Jesus came to peace with his Father's decision. Luke's is the only Gospel to mention that an angel came to strengthen Jesus in that moment. Luke portrays the angel functioning like a trainer who ministers to a wrestler during a tough match.

Having accepted his Father's will, Jesus is able to face the rest of his passion in peace. His real struggle was not with the actual torture, which he endured in silence and without wavering, but in facing and accepting the prospect of his suffering. We, too, often find the prospect of suffering worse than the suffering itself. We are full of anxiety about how we will be able to endure all the things that might happen to us. Once we find ourselves experiencing the pain itself, we somehow discover the strength to get through it. The fact that Jesus had a protracted struggle against fear while in prayer demonstrates to us that we will sometimes have to pray a considerable time before we are able to accept God's will concerning impending suffering.

I will never forget the struggle I had one Thanksgiving night. My father had suffered several heart attacks and he was in danger of death. My mother was having an extremely difficult time coping with the prospect of losing him. After the bleakest Thanksgiving I had ever spent, I could not sleep. I struggled with God a long time over my fear of my father's death and its possible effects on my mother. I pleaded with God not to let him die.

I only became peaceful once I finally admitted that my father's life was totally out of my control. I had no alternative but to trust that God would take care of us no matter what happened. After this, I found the strength to take everything one day at a time. I was able to support others in the family through the ordeal of my father's heart surgery. The worst part of the whole process was that initial struggle to surrender to God's will and trust him as my Father. The peace that resulted made the actual event of the surgery much easier to bear.

The Disciples' Test

Jesus warned the disciples that they too would need to pray if they wanted to survive the impending crisis. However, they did not follow his example of struggling in prayer until peace replaced fear. The disciples could not face their fear and depression and instead gave in to the escape of sleep. Because they did not undergo the struggle to surrender to God's will in the most fearful circumstances, they were thoroughly unprepared when the crisis came crashing in on them.

One can hear the urgency in Jesus' voice when he found them sleeping: "Why do you sleep? Rise and pray that you may not enter into temptation" (Lk 22:46). However, it was too late. They had missed their chance to find strength in prayer. While Jesus was still speaking, the mob appeared to arrest him.

Then the disciples failed miserably. Their first reaction was to strike out with the sword. When Jesus would not permit them to fight on his behalf, the disciples were bewildered and fled. They had none of the calm courage that Jesus had attained from his struggle in prayer.

Even when our spirits are willing, we will not be strong enough to withstand fear unless we pray. When we walk into crises without first letting God strengthen us in prayer, we can expect to fall flat on our faces. It is not easy to be willing to lose our lives. Fear rushes in and overwhelms us, as it did the disciples. Without having had the chance in prayer to cast out fear and come to singleness of heart, we can only follow Jesus half-heartedly, for then fear controls half our heart and in its other half struggles with our love for Jesus.

Because of the disciples' failure, Jesus endured his passion utterly alone. In this, he walked the path we too must walk. Even when we have loving family and friends around us, in the end we each face death alone. No one can accompany us through the gateway of death. We are born alone, naked and crying, and we die alone, stripped of everything, and often in pain. Therefore, like Jesus, we must find our ultimate and secure grounding in God our Father to whom we surrender ourselves and all that we have.

If we do not learn to pray alone with God every day, we will not be ready to face him alone at death or in other crises. A temptation that confronts many Christians who belong to renewal movements is to think that group or liturgical prayer is sufficient. Our best preparation for the loneliness of death is solitude with God in silence, letting him speak to our heart as we quiet our turmoil and busyness. The love and trust this brings gives us the strength to face even our death in peace.

After Peter had failed, Jesus turned and looked at him. As he remembered Jesus' prediction that he would deny him, Peter burst into tears of repentance. Even though he failed Jesus, Peter was full of love for him. In contrast to the self-centered despair of Judas, Peter wept bitterly because he felt he had betrayed his love for Jesus. He was open to forgiveness for his failure. We too can recall times when we failed someone who desperately needed us. We can either turn inward and fall into self-hatred and despair (which do *not* come from the Lord) or we can turn outward, admit what we have done, and weep out of sorrow.

His repentance makes Peter the Rock that can strengthen others later in Acts. It is God's strength, not his own, that makes him the Rock. Peter was frequently reminded how weak he was on his own without God's power. We need to remember this lesson not only regarding ourselves, but also regarding others.

Overview of Luke's Passion Account—Luke 22–23

Reread carefully and slowly the passion account in Luke. The tone of Luke's passion is different from the tone of Mark's. Mark wants us to realize how much Jesus suffered throughout his passion and crucifixion. Although Luke stresses Jesus' suffering in the garden, he focuses on Jesus' subsequent strengthening by his Father to walk through the passion itself with the calm of a martyr.

Luke emphasizes how Jesus suffers without complaint: "As a sheep led to the slaughter or a lamb before its shearer is dumb, so he opens not his mouth. In his humiliation justice was denied him" (Is 53:7-8; Acts 8:32-33). Luke does not mention Jesus' objecting to someone slapping him in the face. Nor do we find the cry on the cross from Mark, "My God, my God, why have you forsaken me?" In Luke, the words of Jesus on the cross reveal a person so strengthened in his own suffering that he can focus on the needs of others. After the soldiers have nailed him to the cross, Jesus prays, "Father, forgive them; for they know not what they do" (23:34). He promises the repentant criminal, "Truly, I say to you, today you will be with me in Paradise" (23:43). Finally, Jesus cries out in a loud voice, saying, "Father, into thy hands I commit my spirit" (23:46), and breathes his last.

Jesus challenges each of us to accept our own suffering and death in peace. Stephen, in Acts, died much like Jesus, forgiving those who killed him and committing his spirit to the Lord. I saw a similar peace and acceptance in my own mother. As most people with cancer, she struggled with the prospect of death. In the early stages of her sickness, she was angry about getting cancer so young. I had the privilege of being with her on her final night and of observing how, despite considerable pain, she had unmistakably come to peace and acceptance. Her very last word, for which she mobilized every remaining bit of energy she had, was "Amen" to a prayer for the dying I had said.

Matthew and Dennis Linn apply Kubler-Ross' five stages in the process of dying to the healing of any memory (overcoming the harmful present effects of painful memories through coming to peace with them in some way). The Linns suggest five stages of forgiveness. These stages are denial, anger, bargaining, depression, and acceptance.[1] Whether we face our final death, or face the smaller "deaths" and hurts earlier in our lifetimes, we need to arrive at the stage of acceptance to find peace. Though not everyone experiences all five stages, each stage represents that with which we typically have to deal anytime we die to something. After denying the problem, anger at being so afflicted, bargaining with God to try to get out of this dying, and depression when all else fails, we finally must come to acceptance of our death. As we reach acceptance of our many "practice deaths," we find strength for greater struggles and ultimately for accepting our final death.

Although Luke's passion account is not as stark as Mark's, he certainly does not downplay the necessity for both Jesus and his followers to be willing to die, even painfully. He does not bypass the need for the cross by putting all his focus on the resurrection, promoting a doctrine of "cheap grace," or a "theology of glory" which views the Christian life as consisting only of joy and consolation. He stresses the need for repentance even by close followers of Jesus, the need to die to ourselves so we can find ourselves, and the need to forgive one another indefinitely.

From Death to Victory—Luke 24

Luke does not conclude his narrative with death. Death is the gateway to glory. In the same way in which Revelation focuses on glory in order to encourage Christians facing suffering and martyrdom for their faith, Luke presents the hope of glory to give us courage to endure our own passion and death. Luke does not emphasize glory out of a superficial understanding of suffering, as some scholars have claimed, but from a conviction that our journey with Jesus does not end with the cross but rather in the Father's home in heaven.

Luke 24 begins with words that apply to us as well as to the women at the tomb: "Why do you seek the living among the dead?" (24:5). We do not seek the living among the dead, but we take heart that the Jesus who died in such torture is now risen and reigning in glory, pouring out his Holy Spirit on us. We do not seek the living among the dead, for we believe that the God who raised Jesus from such a death will also conquer our deaths and raise us up with him.

From our hindsight as Christians, it is hard to comprehend the disciples' shock occasioned by the empty tomb. The Emmaus story in Luke 24:13-35 reconstructs the first disillusionment of the disciples after Jesus' death. Their first thought was not of resurrection but of a stolen body. The disciples needed to hear the risen Jesus explain from Scripture that the Messiah needed to suffer and thus enter glory (Lk 24:26). Only then were they able to comprehend his resurrection.

We, too, need to be steeped in Scripture to understand God's ways. When we face some unexpected crisis, we can only make sense of it as the early Jews and Christians did, by searching the Scriptures to understand how such a matter fits in God's plan. The early Christians were familiar enough with the Scriptures to comb them for insights into their current situation. As we learn God's past ways with his people, we absorb scriptural viewpoints and patterns of how God usually works. The whole of the Scriptures will reveal to us the meaning of our situation.

The only Scriptures that the first Christians had were the Old Testament, for the New Testament had not yet been written. The initial followers of Jesus discovered the meaning of his death and resurrection in the Pentateuch, Prophets, and Psalms. In those sacred books of the Jews they discerned patterns of how God saves his people. They also came to realize that the Messiah was destined to suffer and not only to conquer their oppressors. They had expected the Messiah to be a victorious warrior, slaughtering their enemies. As they looked further, they became aware of a suffering servant, who overcame suffering and death by absorbing it into himself.

The only manner for overcoming death itself is not by killing others, for every one of us still has to die. Christ conquered death itself in the only possible way—by submitting himself to death and then triumphing over it through resurrection. The same is true of our practice deaths. We do not conquer suffering or fear by inflicting them on others, but by surrendering our own fear to God, walking into the practice deaths ourselves, and overcoming them by emerging victoriously through them.

It is also difficult to understand truly horrendous suffering. Sometimes we can endure it only by looking at Christ's passion and by meditating on passages in both the Old and New Testaments about suffering and death. The passion of Jesus and the psalms of suffering seem to offer the only authentic answer to questions like "Why do I have to suffer?" "Why was my spouse killed?" "Why were my innocent children hurt?" "Why did this have to happen?" To such questions, God often gives, not an answer, but peace, as he did to Jesus in the garden.

In Luke 24:36-49, Jesus appears to the disciples gathered together in Jerusalem. His first words are, "Why are you troubled, and why do questionings rise in your hearts?" (24:38). He reconciles them to what has happened and directs their attention forward toward the spread of the gospel in Acts. To reconcile them to the past and to prepare them for the future he relies on their familiarity with the Scriptures.

The risen Jesus used the whole of the Old Testament to understand God's plan—the Law, the Prophets, and the writings. Today, many people want to pick out only supportive biblical passages, rejecting those that do not sustain their present position. We must look, as Jesus did, at the whole of Scripture. If we want to discover God's plan, we search the Bible in the light of the risen Jesus, present in the church and tradition.

Pentecost Changes the Disciples—Acts 2

The disciples had failed Jesus in his passion, for they had not heeded his urging that they pray to receive strength to withstand the test (Lk 22:40,46). However, after his resurrection Jesus forgave them with implied repeated instructions to pray (cf. Lk 24:49; Acts 1:14). When this time they obediently gathered in prayer in the Upper Room, Jesus filled the apostles with his Holy Spirit. By means of the power of the Spirit, the same disciples who had fled at Jesus' passion now confronted both the Jewish crowds and leaders.

In Acts 5:29, the apostles boldly told the Sanhedrin, the Jewish "Supreme Court," that they must obey God rather than human beings. They were beaten, commanded to be silent about Jesus, and released. These men, who had been so afraid of suffering before, now *rejoiced* "that they were accounted worthy to suffer dishonor for the name" (5:41).

In Acts 7:59-60, Stephen, empowered by the Holy Spirit, carries out to death his fearless defense of Christianity before the Sanhedrin. Although he is not one of Jesus' original disciples, Stephen becomes the first to imitate his Lord's example of martyrdom. Luke even implies that Stephen's dying prayer of forgiveness contributed to Saul's change of heart (cf. Acts 7:60–8:1a). After Paul's conversion in Acts 9, the Lord assured the disciple Ananias that Paul was a chosen instrument to carry his Word, "for I will show him how much he must suffer for the sake of my name" (9:16).

If the Spirit enables us to bear witness fearlessly to Jesus' name, rejoicing in any suffering, we can become true martyrs for Jesus. Not only the twelve, but also Stephen, and even Paul, the former persecutor, all witnessed to Jesus when they accepted the power of the Holy Spirit. Today, we can ask for and receive this same power.

SEVEN

Pentecost: Power for Mission and Community

E mpowerment of the disciples by the Holy Spirit launched the church. Let us look at five aspects of this Pentecostal empowerment in Acts: (1) the Holy Spirit as the Father's promise in Acts 1; (2) the outpouring at Pentecost in Acts 2; (3) Peter's inaugural discourse; (4) confirmation from Scripture that Jesus is Christ and Lord; and (5) the response to this outpouring and speech.

The Father's Promise of the Holy Spirit—Acts 1

At the end of Luke's Gospel and again at the beginning of Acts, Jesus instructs the disciples that they must wait together in prayer in Jerusalem before he can send them out on mission (Lk 24:49; Acts 1:4-5). Like Christians of later generations, they were no longer to have the earthly Jesus with them. Moreover, no Christians either then or today would have been able to bring about salvation unless the risen Jesus were with them through his Holy Spirit and through the power of his name.

Acts 1:4-5 identifies the Father's promise with the Holy Spirit. All the expectations of the Old Testament and of God's chosen people, and all their longings and needs, are met by the Holy Spirit. That fulfillment is *not* an earthly kingdom, as many

Jews, including some of the disciples, had expected, even after the resurrection.

In Acts 1:6, the disciples betray this misunderstanding by asking, "Lord, will you at this time restore the kingdom to Israel?" When Jesus had announced the coming of God's kingdom, they apparently assumed this to mean liberation from Roman domination and restoration of their own earthly kingdom as it had been under the reign of David. We should not be surprised at any misinterpretation of the genuine promises of God. Nor should we look down on those who make such mistakes, if even the apostles mistook Jesus' words.

Luke makes it quite clear that God's promises primarily concern not power, material wealth, or security, but his gift of the Holy Spirit and empowerment to live happily and fruitfully in any circumstances. Through the Holy Spirit, we become God's sons and daughters, recipients of an eternal inheritance. Since we are so closely related to our God, who dwells within us, we can trust him for all our material needs. Some may have more possessions, others may have fewer, but our Father provides for the needs of all his children.

The Outpouring at Pentecost—Acts 2:2-13

The disciples awaited the promised gift of the Holy Spirit by gathering in communal prayer in the Upper Room, as Jesus had instructed them. Luke goes out of his way to mention that not only the eleven surviving apostolic leaders were gathered, but an entire community of men and women that numbered "about 120" (1:15). Though not giving an exact head count, he does say "about 120" instead of the more predictable "about 100" or "more than 100."

From Revelation, we appreciate how important number symbolism was in the early church. If Luke were aware of a rule that ten men were needed to constitute a *minyan* or quorum for prayer in the synagogue, the praying community of "about 120" might well symbolize the reconstituted twelve tribes (cf. Lk 22:29-30). However, the 120 persons in Acts would imply some reinterpretation of the rabbinic quorum rules, which insisted on ten *males*. On the contrary, Luke has gone out of his way to mention that the 120 Christians included women.

The Christian prayer quorum is actually two or more persons gathered in Jesus' name (Mt 18:20), but here in Acts 2 the complete Christian community at prayer symbolizes the restored Israel at the time of fulfillment. If the early disciples were like some contemporary religious individualists who insist that they need only Jesus and the Bible, without church or community, there would have been no Pentecost.

Acts 1:14 conspicuously mentions that Mary, the mother of Jesus, was present as a member of the community that awaited Pentecost in prayer. Even Luke, who refers to Mary more than most of the other Gospels, seldom mentions her during Jesus' ministry. However, he refers to her here to demonstrate that just as Mary had received the Holy Spirit so that Jesus could be born, so Mary received the Spirit when the church was born. Peter clearly led the community, but Mary's presence was important at the birth of the church.

Many Catholics who have experienced spiritual renewal through Protestants or who have joined ecumenical prayer groups tend to downplay Mary in their own lives and in their sharing with others. I consider this a tragic mistake. Apart from Jesus himself, no human has ever been as docile to the Father's will as has Mary. No other human was "full of grace," totally free from sin. Nobody else was as Spirit-filled as she was. No one else after Jesus is such a perfect model for the church and for Christians. No other human was as instrumental in bringing about the salvation of us all through the incarnate Son of God, who was also her Son.

Mary was present at the first Pentecost. I believe that she will also play an important role in the new Pentecost for which Pope John XXIII prayed before Vatican II.[1] Both before that council and again more recently, many ordinary Catholics have been more open to God's action through Mary's intercession than through charismatic gifts.

I was surprised in my 1983 retreat to find myself called back to devotion to Mary as mother of the Church and as my mother, as Jesus had made her the mother of his beloved disciple (Jn 19:26-27). I asked her to obtain for me a docility to the Holy Spirit and a union with her Son more like hers. For me, this was also a healing affirmation of the way in which God had worked in my life. In my youth, I was devoted to Mary. I gradually lost awareness of her in the silence about Mary that followed Vatican II. As I returned to her in a new way and even consecrated myself to her as her son (as the beloved disciple was made her son at the cross), I have found a noticeable increase in the gifts and fruits of the Holy Spirit in my life.

In the two decades since then, Mary has become an even more vital part of my everyday living, still more so as I have increased my outreach to Latino Catholics. In the sixteenth century, Our Lady of Guadalupe was responsible for the conversion of millions of Aztecs to Catholicism. At the turn of the millennium, Pope John Paul II has declared her patroness of the Americas. In addition, because the Guadalupe image portrays Mary as pregnant, Catholics in the pro-life movement have become especially devoted to Our Lady of Guadalupe.

The coming of the Holy Spirit on the church parallels the coming of the Holy Spirit on Jesus in Luke 3:21-22. Both Jesus and the community were in prayer when this coming occurred. After receiving the Spirit, both Jesus and Peter gave their "inaugural address" (Lk 4:16-30; Acts 2:14-36), which set forth the mission to be carried out in the rest of each book.

Wind and fire signified the coming of the Holy Spirit. Old Testament Hebrew uses the same word for both spirit and wind; so does New Testament Greek. The combination of wind and fire comes from the Old Testament prophetic symbolism of the wind separating wheat from chaff and the fire burning the chaff. The Baptist's image of baptizing with wind and fire (Lk 3:16) is, therefore, a symbol of judgment separating good from evil. It is the same notion that Simeon voiced to Mary in the temple (Lk 2:34-35).

In Acts, Luke reinterprets John's prophecy about the baptism of Spirit and fire, putting less stress on judgment and purification and more on empowerment. After this experience of wind and fire, the disciples no longer feared to admit they were followers of Jesus. The Holy Spirit always gives people the courage to witness to their faith.

Since the mid-1960s, a major revival of the gift of speaking in tongues has taken place in Catholic and mainline Protestant churches as well as among Pentecostal Christians. Many Christians from all denominational backgrounds were again introduced to the experience of this gift of the Holy Spirit, which seems to have lain dormant for so long in most of

Western Christendom. Tongues has proven to be an effective gateway to spiritual freedom and to other gifts of the Spirit such as healing, prophecy, visions, and deliverance from evil spirits.

Acts 2 describes a missionary phenomenon in which many people who spoke different languages heard the same speakers, each in their own language. Acts interprets the tongues at Pentecost in the light of the quotation from Joel 3:1-5, which promises that God will pour out his Spirit on all flesh and they shall *prophesy*. While prophecy is intelligible, most speaking in tongues is not (see 1 Cor 14). The tongues at Pentecost were intelligible and helped convert many.

On the other hand, in 1 Corinthians 12–14, Paul limits the use of tongues in public gatherings and encourages more prophecy instead, precisely because the hearers cannot understand tongues. He calls tongues "languages of men and angels," and he implies that the angelic tongues, at least, are not human languages. The way in which most Christians experience tongues today, moreover, is closer to Paul's description of them than to the account of Pentecost. Although some people claim to have heard a variety of human languages that were unknown to the one who was speaking in tongues, that phenomenon seems to be a special gift related to evangelization—a sign to attract unbelievers.

At my first introduction to the gift of tongues, I was repelled. Since I had never read anything about tongues, the phenomenon seemed like senseless babbling. I realized that I needed the Holy Spirit, but I made it very clear that I did not want tongues. The priest who prayed with me said I should not tell the Holy Spirit what he could or could not do with me. I agreed to pray for the Holy Spirit, and, if God wanted also to give me tongues, to accept that gift.

The gift of tongues has proven to be an extremely important gift of the Spirit for my own spiritual growth. It opened me up to surrendering control and submitting to God in something that made no intellectual sense to me. It has been a very important lesson in surrender, in letting God work in unexpected ways. It reminds me in practice of what I know in theory, that God's ways are not our ways (Is 55:8).

The gift of tongues is a way of allowing the Holy Spirit to pray in us when we do not know how to pray (cf. Rm 8:26). With tongues, our praise of God does not run out of language, in contrast to our limited number of English expressions of praise. I have also found the gift of tongues invaluable when I had to minister to people in immense suffering or deep trouble. In addition, I have also witnessed prayer in tongues stop oppression of people by evil spirits.

The power in tongues springs from the surrender we make to the Holy Spirit. Whether or not Paul was thinking of tongues in Romans 8:26-27, his words certainly apply also to praying in tongues:

> Likewise the Spirit helps us in our weakness; for we do not know how to pray as we ought, but the Spirit himself intercedes for us with sighs too deep for words. And he who searches the hearts of men knows what is the mind of the Spirit, because the Spirit intercedes for the saints according to the will of God.

Because God's Holy Spirit is himself interceding for us from within us, God will certainly answer his own prayer on our behalf!

Even if charismatic renewal has directly influenced only a

small percentage of Catholics, I believe that God's charismatic gifts are somehow meant for the whole church, not only for some fringe group. God's charismatic gifts enable him to work much more freely in our liturgies, sacraments, preaching, healing prayer, and all kinds of ministry. In charismatic gifts such as tongues and prophecy, God retains control of what happens, whereas in so much of parish life and worship, we humans try to control everything.

The charismatic gifts challenge us all to let God be in charge of his church. Let God anoint our homilies. Let God speak to the whole church in prophecy. Let God sweep up the whole congregation in powerful praise of his glory through our lips in tongues. Let God work miraculous healings as we pray for one another in expectant faith that the sick will be healed. Let God guide our parish council decisions as we stop our ceaseless talk, activity, planning, and politics, and listen together for his guidance in prayer. Let God and not pressure groups or ideologues set the priorities and agendas of our dioceses.

A very important and common gift of God's Holy Spirit relates to Scripture. The Bible begins to speak powerfully to us when we ask God in faith to address us personally or as a community. This gift is not the exclusive province of those who have experienced charismatic gifts, but is common to many who have turned to Scripture for direction in their own lives. When we open ourselves to biblical guidance, God through his inspired word in Scripture can give us perspective on any issue or moral question that arises. This openness is especially important at a time when many are trying to censor, rewrite, or radically reinterpret Scripture in order to downplay its authority over the church and our own lives today.

People who have personally experienced how Scripture has

freed them and changed their lives when they submitted their own views to its authority are often labeled "fundamentalists" because they are slow to dismiss biblical principles in deference to some contemporary ideology. However, it is not fundamentalism to take God's Word seriously and to try to practice it. It is not fundamentalism to recognize that God's ways are different from ours and to refrain from dismissing entire biblical themes and texts as "time-bound" or "culturally conditioned" simply because they challenge our contemporary cultural conditioning.

To be truly open to the Holy Spirit, Catholics must accept God's revelation as he has given it in Scripture, fostered it in tradition, and protected it, by the teaching authority of the church, from misinterpretation.[2] We must acknowledge God's revelation as he continues to apply it to our own contemporary circumstances.

The reception of the Holy Spirit at Pentecost marked the beginning of the church. Reception of the same Spirit continues to be necessary to revivify the church today. As the Holy Spirit gave to the first Christians the gifts the church needed, so today the Spirit is giving us gifts that the church needs.

Some of God's gifts surprise us, challenge our preconceptions, and make us uncomfortable. Nevertheless, once we are sure they are from God, who are we to denigrate them and refuse to allow them in our parishes? An attitude of submission to God requires us to put aside personal preferences or dislikes. Who are we, the clay, to tell the divine Potter how to mold us (cf. Is 64:8; Jer 18:6)?

Students have asked why, after so many centuries of lying dormant, charismatic gifts such as tongues should suddenly have become so visible in the churches in recent decades. History offers possible parallels. In the 1600s, the Catholic

Church suffered from the heresy called Jansenism, which caused people to doubt that they were worthy of God's love. Jansenism aroused an unreasonable fear of God's judgment and a spirit of negativity. People avoided the Eucharist because they felt unworthy to receive Christ. God's response to Jansenism was to raise up a new devotion in the Church, a devotion to Christ's tender love as symbolized by his Sacred Heart. Even some of its more sentimental manifestations were beneficial for countering the cold, judgmental rationalism of Jansenism.

Since the Enlightenment and modernism, the heresy of deism has infiltrated much contemporary theology and religious education, in both Protestant and Catholic churches. It may be that the recent unexpected increase in charismatic gifts such as tongues, prophecies, and healings is God's answer to the deism of so much modern theology. Today, through the very miracles that deists deny are possible, God counters the deistic disbelief that he will intervene in our lives or answer our prayers.

By charismatic and other interventions, God is also undermining the secular humanism of any deism that puts all its emphasis on human projects and ideologies. In addition, he is giving the lie to a postmodern deconstruction that is now exceeding even the reductionism of modernistic deism, when it degrades the status of religious words and claims to nothing more than raw ideological use of power. God is showing our generation that he not only has power to act in our lives, but that he will gladly intervene with that power when we ask him to.

In Pentecost and in the outpouring of his Holy Spirit today, God shows himself to be a God of surprises. He is too much for our narrow categories, ideologies, and expectations. God is showing that he continues to be a God of signs and wonders, as Scripture portrays him.

Peter's Speech at Pentecost—Acts 2:14-21

Signs and wonders such as the Pentecost phenomena are not proofs, nor are they self-explanatory. In Acts 2, Peter explains the meaning of the Pentecost tongues, and in Acts 3, what the healing of the lame man signifies. This precedent is very important for explaining signs and wonders that happen today. For ordinary people to understand healing and spiritual gifts such as tongues, we need to account for them in the light of Scripture and God's promises, as Peter did in Acts.

The mixed reactions of the crowd to tongues at Pentecost imply that the manifestations needed such explanation. Some of the crowd thought the disciples were drunk (their reaction might suggest that they heard tongues as unintelligible babbling), while others heard speech in their own languages. Still others refused to be impressed in either case. The very same sign touched the hearts of some people but hardened those of others, so that they scoffed at the phenomenon.

Even impressive signs leave people free to believe or disbelieve them, and require some explanation and interpretation. For instance, even the resurrection was a sign that required Jesus' explanation before the disciples could understand it. In addition, even if we have heard the interpretation of a sign, to believe or not still remains a freely chosen act. The most powerful signs of God will not convince us if we do not want to believe.

In the same way, we cannot prove to others that we love them. We can only give them signs of our love, concern, and protection. However, every sign can be counterfeited. Jealousy (a form of unbelief) can frustrate us. We cannot convince a jealous spouse that we love them. Signs can demonstrate that someone loves us only if we *believe* that the signs are genuine.

In like manner, we have to believe that signs in our lives show us God's love. This is what "salvation by faith" implies: to accept and receive God's love and forgiveness we must believe in it. To break down our fear and resistance, God and others can only give us repeated signs of their love for us.

In his speech in Acts 2, Peter explains the signs and wonders of Pentecost. As Jesus' speech at Nazareth in Luke 4:16-30 did for the Gospel, Peter's speech establishes the program for the entire ministry to come in the Acts of the Apostles. Further, the citation from Joel 2:28-32 in Acts 2:17-21 provides a special key to understanding the Acts.

In the time immediately before Christ, various groups had diverse expectations about how God would bring about his kingdom. Some expectations included a Messiah, and others did not. Nevertheless, the prophecies about God's final out-pouring of his Spirit were prominent in most first-century sce-narios of the final days.

Joel predicted that in the time of fulfillment God would give his Spirit to all men and women, not just to a few select prophets and kings. All people would have direct access to God, be able to speak God's Word, and receive God's revelation in visions and dreams. In the final days, God would work mar-velous signs and wonders, as he did when he saved the Israelites from Egyptian slavery. Luke claims that the coming of the Spirit at Pentecost and his work in Christians throughout the rest of Acts fulfills the deepest longings and expectations for salvation of the Jewish people.

This central Lukan theme has very important implications for today. Some Christians can fail to see the continuity between God's action in the Old Testament and his action in the New.

They can make a comparable mistake in their own lives by rejecting all that went before their extraordinary experience of the Spirit's gifts. God did not begin to act in our lives when he filled us, as adults, with powerful gifts of his Spirit. He has been working in us all along, preparing us for the fullness of his Spirit.

Thus, when we receive the gifts of the Holy Spirit, we are not to despise or neglect the previous gifts of nature that God has given us. We do not despise wisdom that we gained from previous experience. We do not automatically reject friends and relatives that God gave us before our experience of conversion. We do not downgrade the educational and cultural gifts God gave to others and to us and become anti-intellectual boors in the name of the Holy Spirit.

The same Luke who puts such emphasis on the new action and gifts of the Holy Spirit also stresses their continuity with God's action and preparation in the Old Testament. The Holy Spirit, foretold through the prophets, now begins our journey on the Christian way, leading us through its many turns, empowering us to work signs in Jesus' name, and enabling us to give fearless witness to him.

In Luke 12:11-12, Jesus had directed his disciples not to be anxious when they were dragged before authorities, or to worry about what to say, "for the Holy Spirit will teach you in that very hour what you ought to say." Jesus' promise is fulfilled when, at different times, Peter, John, Stephen, and Paul are filled with the Holy Spirit to answer charges in court.

Once, with a friend at his divorce trial, I got a glimpse of the terror that people experience when they expect to be called to the witness stand and to be attacked in every conceivable way by a hostile, skilled attorney. They cannot sleep the night before. They often get sick before going to court. If a divorce trial can cause this much fear, what must the disciples have faced when on trial for their lives? Jesus tells them and us to be at peace when facing a trial. We are not to rehearse, anxiously and endlessly, what we are to say, for the Holy Spirit will give us words to say when the time comes.

Proof From Scripture and the Empty Tomb— Acts 2:22-36

Peter begins his explanation of the phenomena of Pentecost by citing the prophecy in Joel of the outpouring of the Spirit. His explanation links this quotation from Joel with what happened to Jesus. In contrast to the expectations of the chosen people, the Jesus whom they rejected initiated this final age of the Holy Spirit. God had already given them witness to Jesus by the mighty works, wonders, and signs he had done through Jesus in their presence. Now God has vindicated Jesus after the people have had him crucified by the Romans. Peter's explanation shows that all this happened according to God's plan and in fulfillment of the prophecies of David in the Psalms (16 and 110).

When we are faced with unexpected traumas such as the crucifixion or awesome signs such as those of Pentecost, the first Christians provide a model for us. They sought explanations in God's revelation of his plan in Scripture and in events. Faith is not merely a blind leap, as some say. Faith also seeks understanding. We need to know how our experience relates to the ways in which God has saved his people, and we need arguments by which to defend and make sense of our faith when it is challenged.

Acts 2 provides a proof that despite all the contrary evidence of Jesus' crucifixion, God has made him both Messiah and Lord. A proof is no substitute for faith; we still must choose to believe or not, but the proof can make some sense of our choice to believe. A proof can be an incentive to others to make the same act of faith as we did.

Acts 2 provides a theological argument based on both Scripture and experience. Though theology cannot match the power of signs and wonders to touch hearts and change lives, it has an important function: it explains those signs and wonders in relation to God's previous revelation. It helps us to distinguish between competing claims and signs by determining which come from God and which do not. It helps to explain to others our choices to believe and can remove obstacles so they too can believe.

The Lukan argument in Acts 2 hinges on the identity of the one who, Psalm 16 predicted, would not see corruption. The person about whom this prophecy was made cannot be David because his tomb remains occupied; therefore, the one foretold must be the Messiah, who is a descendant of David. The apostles are witnesses that God raised Jesus from the dead. Therefore, God has established Jesus as Messiah.

The argument depends completely on the fact that Jesus' tomb was discovered empty. Though the significance of the empty tomb may seem obvious, many have recently begun teaching or preaching that the empty tomb is not important for our faith. It has become quite popular in theological and religious-education circles to give a more "sophisticated" interpretation of resurrection that sees no problem in admitting that Jesus' bones remain in his grave.

Of course, the empty tomb by itself does not prove that Jesus rose from the dead, since it is possible for the body to have been removed or stolen. The Emmaus account in Luke 24 also indicates that the empty tomb alone did not convince even the disciples that Jesus had risen. However, the resurrection was to be a *sign* to the ordinary people who made up the early church. A sign must be comprehensible to the people to whom it is given. Even if some sophisticated turn-of-the-millennium theologians can conceive of a resurrection without an empty tomb, that notion would have been nonsense to ordinary people at the time of Christ.

First-century Jews and Christians were aware of the concepts both of resurrection from the dead and of immortality of the soul. In their minds, these were two different concepts. A widespread Greek worldview tended to stress immortality of the soul, and to despise the body, thus rejecting any notion of resurrection of the body. A familiar Jewish approach (in Daniel and 2 Maccabees) stressed a restoration of the whole embodied person through bodily resurrection.[3]

For the ordinary person, the word "resurrection" presupposed that something would happen to the dead body, so that it would no longer remain dead. To disprove Christian talk about resurrection, the Jews would have needed only to point to Jesus' body still in the tomb. We are historically certain the Jews never did this, although second-century Jewish texts did charge that the Christians had stolen Jesus' body.

The empty tomb was critically important to the first Christians. Without it, they might presume that Jesus' appearances were hallucinations or ghosts. The empty tomb is also important today for faith in the resurrection. I am convinced that scholarly objections to the empty tomb come not from the evidence of the New Testament, but from difficulty in accepting God's miraculous intervention in our lives and the very possibility or meaning of bodily resurrection.

The People's Response—Acts 2:37-41

Peter's explanation of the signs and wonders of Pentecost and his argument that Jesus really is the Messiah cut the crowd to the heart. They ask, "What shall we do?"

We have here another precedent for the church today. Preaching should touch people's hearts and ready them for conversion. Our preaching must not result merely from our human preparation but from the Holy Spirit. It ought to receive its power from the preachers' personal experience and witness. It should reason from Scripture to make sense of that experience in the light of these truths. Thus, Peter's personal witness that Jesus was the awaited Messiah touched his hearers. Merely reading canned homilies purchased from liturgical publishers will hardly lead to conversions.

Giving our personal witness to people about the truths of the faith and to Jesus as Messiah and Lord does touch them, however. We do not water down our preaching about Christ or morality simply because people do not believe or are living in immoral situations. As Peter shows, we can speak the truth in love and let the listeners come to grips with any discrepancy between the teaching and their own lives and behavior. Good preaching *should* sometimes unsettle the hearers and challenge them to deal with the difference between God's ways and theirs. It should persuade them to ask, "What shall we do?"

Preaching differs from personal counseling. Preaching must hold up the ideal. It should proclaim God's ways without compromise. When this kind of preaching triggers guilt in listeners, personal counseling can help them to sort out practical options for their particular situations.

Peter's speech also illustrates the difference between "convicting" and "condemning." To convict hearers is to tell them that they have done wrong, and to arouse them to receive forgiveness and to change. Condemning one's listeners only leads them to guilt and hopeless despair. Thus, when unbelievers feel convicted of wrongdoing and ask what they should do, we say with Peter:

> Repent, and be baptized every one of you in the name of Jesus Christ for the forgiveness of your sins; and you shall receive the gift of the Holy Spirit. For the promise is to you and to your children and to all that are far off [i.e., not only to the chosen people but to all nations], every one whom the Lord our God calls to him.
>
> ACTS 2:38-39

To Christians who have sinned, we say, "Repent and confess your sins in Jesus' name for the forgiveness of your sins." Catholics and other Christians who practice the sacrament of reconciliation confess their sins verbally to the minister designated by the church.

The acute decline in the use of this sacrament by Catholics since Vatican II has proven to be a very grave loss to the Church and its people. People today sin as seriously as they did decades ago, when confessions were common. Catholics who sin seriously still have the obligation to confess their sins to a priest before presenting themselves for communion, though they often seem unaware of this obligation. Today, we often find the scandalous situations of cohabiting or other unmarried people who are known to have had illicit sexual intercourse during the preceding week but who receive the Eucharist on Sunday without confession. Parishes need to address the scandal of sacrilegious and blasphemous reception of the Eucharist by people known to be living in serious sin who have no intention of changing their way of life.

Every individual has the personal obligation to choose to believe the good news, to receive baptism, and to confess sins for forgiveness. God saves us as individuals, but God does not leave us isolated as saved and forgiven individuals. He calls us into community with others whom Jesus has reconciled with his Father.

Acts demonstrates that the first Christians did not go off alone with their Bibles. Instead, they "were added" to the Christian community of 3,000 people. They assented to their reconciliation and salvation as individuals, but they joined the church to live and worship with others whom God had saved.

Acts 2:42-47 demonstrates the ideal for our Christian lives together as God's church. As believers, we are to share our lives and even our goods as we unite with other Christians. God may not call everyone to hold their goods in common: some early communities in Acts did not have goods in common (e.g., at Ephesus, Acts 20:32-35). Nevertheless, God calls all of us to share materially as well as spiritually with our brothers and sisters in Christ.

EIGHT

The Christian Way Is for All Peoples

The outpouring of the Holy Spirit in Acts 2 not only converted individuals but also formed Christian community in
Jerusalem. Acts 2–5 describe the development and growth of
this community of converted Jews. In Acts 6–7, the first church
at Jerusalem begins to take in new classes of people as leaders.
In Acts 8, the disciples begin to evangelize others besides pure
Jews, the "half-breed" Samaritans. Acts 10–11 and 15 describe
the major turning point in early Christian history—Christians
begin to admit uncircumcised non-Jews into the church without forcing them first to become circumcised as Jews. This
reception of uncircumcised Gentiles is a paradigm or model for
the challenge Jesus gives us today to invite new kinds of people
to join us on our Christian way.

Expansion of Community—Acts 6–8

The church began with a dedicated community of converted
Jews in Jerusalem. These new Christians found strength in their
union in community around the apostles. However, one of the
dangers of any community is that it can become exclusive or too
comfortable with one type of people and one way of doing
things. Exclusiveness in community can be a kind of spiritual
hoarding. In contrast, hospitality toward new people helps to

keep a community's close, committed relationships healthy. In our gratitude for the tremendous blessings that God has given us, we are eager to share them with others by inviting new people to join us.

Already in Acts 6, Luke describes friction in the church in Jerusalem between two types of Jews, whom he names "Hebrews" and "Hellenists." The Hebrews were the Jews who spoke primarily Aramaic, the primary language of the ordinary people in Palestine. Aramaic was closely related to Hebrew, the language of the Jewish Bible. The Hellenists were Jews who spoke primarily Greek, the international language since about 300 B.C. The Hellenists were also formed especially by Greek culture as adapted by Mediterranean and Near Eastern peoples.

Thus, the Jewish Christian church in Jerusalem was bilingual and bicultural. These Christians experienced some of the misunderstandings common to other such bilingual groups. We find similar frictions between French-speaking and English-speaking Canadians, or, in some cities of the U.S., between Latinos and Anglos. The more recent or less influential group tends to feel discrimination: "Now in these days when the disciples were increasing in number, the Hellenists murmured against the Hebrews because their widows were neglected in the daily distribution" (Acts 6:1).

Acts 6 provides a beautiful example of how to handle such frictions between majority and minority groups in a community. The twelve realized that the increasing size of the community was making it difficult for them to be able to serve the needs of all the members, especially of those who had joined the church more recently and whom they knew less well. They solved the problem by surrendering some of their exclusive authority and control over all aspects of the growing community's life.

Because the twelve had to retain overall leadership and their symbolic status over the twelve tribes of the restored Israel, they did not add to their number and become "the nineteen," but they formed a new group, "the seven."

Delegating the distribution of community goods and services to the party whose members had felt slighted exhibited an impressive act of trust by the twelve. They did not simply add some token minority members to the crew who were already responsible for distributing community resources, but put members of the minority group in charge of that entire process. Nor, despite the first impression given by the narrative, did these new members of the leadership team merely "wait on tables" or handle material matters while the twelve took care of everything spiritual. Acts 6–8 demonstrate that the Holy Spirit filled Stephen and Philip with power and wisdom that empowered them to evangelize, preach, and work signs and wonders much as the twelve did.

Control over the community purse can symbolize authority over the community (Acts 4:34-37). Control of the purse by the seven symbolizes their authority in all the basic aspects of running the community, from Stephen's defense of Christians against the attacks of outsiders to Philip's evangelizing new members. The Spirit anointed the seven as well as the twelve to witness, preach, heal, and act as leaders. Stephen, a member of the seven, had the privilege of being the first to die for Jesus (Acts 7:60), even before James, one of the twelve, gave his life (Acts 12:2).

Persecution after Stephen's death drove all these Hellenists out of Jerusalem, but not the apostles (Acts 8:1). God used this persecution to expand the church through the exiled Hellenist leaders. When Philip evangelized Samaria (Acts 8), the church made its first step toward incorporating others than Jews in good standing.

The Acts of the Apostles repeatedly emphasizes this precedent, that God works through failure in one situation to divert us toward a new one. Rejection and persecution result from unsuccessful evangelizing; they imply failures to persuade. Yet God repeatedly moved Paul to evangelize new cities when cities that he had previously evangelized rejected his message and drove him out.

Similarly, God today frequently works in our lives through events that we experience as failures. He often closes doors to one work or one area in order to get us to choose a different occupation or to go elsewhere. No one likes to have doors closed in his face. Yet, when God does permit a door to be closed on us, we do not stand there and keep pounding on it— we move on toward the next opportunity. God works for our good in *everything* (Rom 8:28, 38-39).

Cleansing Gentiles From Idolatry and Immorality— Acts 10–11, 15

Acts 10–11 and 15 describe a turning point. Early Christianity was now expanding from a Jewish movement to one that included non-Jews. In these chapters, Luke describes also the issues involved.

These narratives provide models for contemporary evangelization. Both the early and the present-day church have struggled with how to incorporate people from newly evangelized cultures. What would new converts have to give up from their own cultures and backgrounds in order to become Christians?

In turn, what adaptations should Christianity make to the cultures of potential converts to eliminate unnecessary obstacles to conversion? As theologians express the controversy today, how much should the gospel be "inculturated" within a particular culture, and how much should it challenge the culture it enters?

The key to interpreting chapters 10–11 and 15 is Peter's "food" vision in Acts 10:9-16. Like many contemporary dreams and visions, Peter's was symbolic. Despite first impressions, the vision was not about eating unclean food. The point was, "What God has cleansed, you must not call common" (10:15).

Acts 10:28 applied this saying to humans, not to food: "But God has shown me I should not call any man common or unclean." God emphasizes this lesson by cleansing the "unclean" Gentiles with the Holy Spirit before anyone could circumcise them (Acts 10:44-48). Peter answered the unsurprising objections of Jewish Christians against baptizing uncircumcised Gentiles this way: "If then God gave the same gift to them as he gave to us when we believed in the Lord Jesus Christ, who was I that I could withstand God?" (11:17).

It is hard today to appreciate the depth and meaning of the Jewish anxiety over uncleanness in these chapters. Flavius Josephus, a Jewish historian roughly contemporary with Luke, reflects Jewish sensitivities in his time when he calls Gentiles "profane men" to whom the divine realities of Jewish law and practice should not be disclosed (*Jewish Antiquities* 12:112). Even sayings attributed to Jesus exemplify this view: "Do not throw your pearls before swine" (Mt 7:6), and "It is not right to take the children's bread and throw it to the dogs" (Mk 7:27).

The requirement that one be cleansed and rendered fit to enter the divine presence is common in most of the world's religions. The truth is that God is holy, and unholiness is unworthy of him. This ancient religious sensibility embodies a respect for God's holiness that people today often lack. However, religious awe is deep in the human psyche, and most God-fearing people have felt it.

Both the disciples in Acts and Jesus in the Gospels seem to challenge this sensitivity by welcoming unclean Gentiles and sinners. Association with the "unclean" caused extensive friction between Jesus and religious leaders. Jesus reached out to unclean lepers, to a woman unclean with a flow of blood, to tax collectors who collaborated with unclean Roman Gentiles, to unclean dead people, and to people with unclean spirits.

Both Jesus and the church in Acts evangelized the "unclean" (Lk 5:31-32). However, when Jesus reached out to the unclean, he did not leave them in their uncleanness. He cleansed the leper, healed the woman with the flux, raised the dead to life, and drove out unclean spirits. The early church also expected converts from paganism to leave their previous pagan ways and live a new, holy kind of life (e.g., Eph 4:17–5:20). Acts 15 allows inculturation but only within limits.

The two main changes required in Acts of converts from paganism were respect for some Jewish dietary prescriptions and avoidance of any immoral acts from their previous lives as pagans. Without a compromise regarding these dietary prescriptions, converts to Christianity from Judaism and paganism would not be able to share common meals and the Eucharist. Many of the earliest Christians continued to be practicing Jews and would find it hard to unite in the same community with those who violated Jewish laws concerning food. Even today, orthodox Jews must eat in a kosher setting.

In Jewish eyes, the practice of idolatry is what most rendered pagans unclean. By the time of Jesus, Jews considered pagan gods to be unclean spirits, as in Paul's explanation in 1 Corinthians 10:18-21. Paul and other Jews and Christians did not simply dismiss pagan gods as nonentities or idolatry as harmless nonsense. Idolatrous practices did have an effect on people, as do occult practices today.

Because some idolatrous practices were self-evidently immoral in Jewish eyes (e.g., human sacrifice and cult prostitution), Jews did not maintain that pagans were simply worshipping the true God in ignorance. In their view, immoral practices pointed to immoral "gods," that is, to evil spirits. Worship of such unclean spirits rendered pagans unclean and unable to worship God. One cannot have relationships with both unclean spirits and the Holy Spirit.[1]

Jews and Christians were especially outspoken against pagan sexual immorality (i.e., adultery, fornication, homosexual practices, prostitution, abortion, and infanticide). In addition to being evidently contrary to the will of God as made clear in Scripture, sexual immorality threatens the family, the basic unit of any community. Christians did not accept "alternate lifestyles" that would put families with unmarried parents or homosexual couples on a par with husband, wife, and children.

Thus early Christians did not try to render less onerous through permissiveness those life situations that seemed to be insoluble, such as the circumstances of single parents or of those attracted to the same sex who had little hope of ordinary marriage and family. Through the power of the Holy Spirit and the support of Christian community, Christian compassion is able to help and to heal people when medical and psychological means have failed. There are no completely hopeless alcoholics, hopelessly compulsive homosexuals,[2] or hopelessly promiscuous heterosexuals. The God who raises from the dead can heal any condition. The Holy Spirit can change anyone. Christian community can provide the support such people need to be able to change at least their behavior.

Through the years, Alcoholics Anonymous has illustrated the power of God and community to control the most "hopeless" compulsions. They have insisted that the alcoholic first admit that he or she is alcoholic and stop denying the problem. They have reached out in compassion to other alcoholics as fellow alcoholics, rather than from a position of superiority. They have been available any hour of the day or night to help someone outlast a temptation to drink.

They have exhorted alcoholics to rely on God's power, not their own, to transform them. They have demonstrated to fellow alcoholics what they call "tough love." Their tough love confronts lies and manipulation, does not enable or cover over drinking, and challenges alcoholics to change destructive behavior in order to attain sobriety. It is not an act of love to make it easier for the alcoholic to get the drink that will kill him.

Similarly, it is not true love to be permissive about sexual or other compulsions that ruin people's lives and trap them in situations that cause misery, allow tremendous abuse, or undermine the traditional family. Christians can reach out with tough but generous love and support to such people. We can also pray that the Spirit heal and empower change in them.

On occasion God has been known to actually change the psychological or physical causes of the problem, for example, by diverting homosexual energies back into heterosexual channels. When God does not make such an extraordinary change, he can still enable the persons to live tranquil, chaste, and happy lives while remaining as they are. We can tell people the good news that God can free them from their compulsions and enable them to live sober and peaceful lives of self-control. We can challenge them to accept God's help and choose to change. We can support and help them live with their behavior transformed.

Jesus and the early church combined compassion for sinners with a challenge to stop sinning. We cannot deny how difficult it is in today's environment to live the New Testament morality, yet we solve nothing by watering down the requirements of living as Christians. Rather than permissiveness, our church especially needs greater openness to the power of the Holy Spirit.

Under the Spirit's guidance and empowerment, the church also needs to build genuine communities among the faithful and not merely anonymous parishes. A setting of supportive community that exercises the healing gifts of the Spirit enables Christians to live New Testament moral ideals even today. Alcoholics Anonymous unmistakably demonstrates that mere willpower is not enough to overcome alcoholism. Without God's empowerment and the help of community, people will continue to stagger under the burden of their sins as they fall short of the New Testament ideals of love and self-control.

New Testament communities helped believers live the Christian way. If a spouse or parents died, the church took care of the widows and orphans. The church provided for members in extreme need. The church did not lay heavy burdens on people without lifting a hand to help carry them.

If their efforts to obey the Catholic teaching against artificial birth control sometimes leave families short of resources, Christian community should help them. When a divorced person finds it painful to live alone and not to remarry, community support can help raise the children, provide missing father or mother figures, and give family-type support to the single parent. Community can help people struggling with abuse of alcohol or overeating by providing families with which to live and by helping them make a new start.

Strong committed parishes or communities are needed to do such things, but the early church had them, and we, too, should make them a top priority. Rather than give in to all sorts of pressure groups seeking permissiveness for people in challenging situations, we as Jesus' church should build communities strong enough to make living as Christians not only possible but also peaceful.

The Struggle to Accept a Change of Direction—Acts 10

Peter had tremendous difficulty understanding and accepting the radical new approach of baptizing unclean pagans without first circumcising them. Therefore it took three versions of the same vision to get through to him in Acts 10:9-16. Three times Peter saw a sheet with animals on it. Each time a voice told him to kill and eat, but Peter protested he had never eaten anything unclean. The voice responded each time, "What God has cleansed, you must not call common" (10:15). If we receive the same vision three times, we will certainly not forget it. This vision burned itself into Peter's consciousness, even though he did not yet understand it.

We need to remember what a reversal of Peter's previous religious training this vision implied. All his life, he had been taught to eat only kosher food, as a way of expressing his membership in God's holy people. Now the vision was telling him not to call unclean what God has cleansed. Peter had a hard time accepting God's new message because he could not see how it corresponded to God's previous revelations. God confirmed this vision by presenting it three times, and then by having the messengers from Cornelius arrive and set in motion the events that would explain to Peter the meaning of the vision.

The Spirit told Peter, still perplexed over his triple vision, not to hesitate to go with the Gentiles. The Spirit told him, in effect, to mingle with the "unclean," since God had sent them. Therefore, Peter went with them. Acts 10:28-29 explains the meaning of the vision:

> You yourselves know how unlawful it is for a Jew to associate with or to visit any one of another nation; but God has shown me that I should not call any man common or unclean. Therefore, when I was sent for, I came without objection.

After Peter preached a summary of the good news to them (Acts 10:34-43), and before anyone could circumcise them, God gave his Holy Spirit to the Gentiles as he had to the disciples at Pentecost. They spoke in tongues as the disciples had. "Can any one forbid water for baptizing these people who have received the Holy Spirit just as we have?" (10:47).

Sometimes we find ourselves faced with changes in the church or in our life that bother us. They seem to go against what we have been taught. Suddenly the Mass that was supposed to be in Latin is now in English. Catholics used to be warned not to touch the host, and now we receive it in the hand. Women, previously forbidden in the sanctuary, are now giving out communion. Are we to doubt what we have been taught before? If the Church was wrong before, how can we trust what it teaches now? Sometimes changes can raise sincere questions of faith.

As we ponder over changes that perplex us, we must recognize that some, like those above, are God's will for a new situation. As Peter had to adjust to the new situation in which God gave his Spirit directly to uncircumcised and unclean pagans, so we must adjust to the ways in which God adapts his church to new situations today. As we continue to listen to God, we understand new circumstances or get new interpretations of older truths. It can console us to see in Acts that Peter and the early church had to make similar marked changes and adjustments in their thinking and practice.

On the other hand, as we ponder other changes in teaching and practice, we may observe that they are not really God's will but aberrations. We determine whether changes are God's will or aberrations by checking them against God's Word in Scripture and against the official teaching of the church. Pope John Paul II has given an example of such discernment. He has clearly condemned certain liturgical abuses and certain political activities on the part of religious and priests. He has explicitly condemned the new forms of permissiveness in sex. He, like Peter, has learned to affirm some changes, and to condemn others.

Though the New Testament frequently warns us against false teachings and teachers, it also often shows us that we may have to change our perspective if we wish to move with God as he moves in his church. As followers of God's Spirit, we can neither keep everything in rigid and unchanging categories, nor be swept by every wind of change. We need to discern when God is moving.

Following the Spirit is a genuine risk: we could make mistakes. Fear of heresy and error should not prevent us from changing when God wants us to change. Peter took an enormous risk in letting pagans be baptized. He was sharply criticized for doing this. If Peter had refused to listen to God's new revelations to him in prayer, he would never have reached out to the Gentiles. Peter's example shows us that we cannot live only by what was set down in the past. We must listen to the Holy Spirit speaking today as well.

Peter's Speech and the Aftermath—Acts 10:34–11:17

Peter instructs the household of Cornelius that God shows no partiality (Dt 10:17); he accepts any people of any nation who believe in him and act rightly (Acts 10:34-35). At the end of his speech, in 10:43, Peter applies this same impartiality to the Christian message: everyone who believes in Jesus as judge of the living and dead receives forgiveness of sins in his name. Peter's message addresses the problem of racial and other kinds of prejudice. To exclude people from our groups without justification is to exclude God's own sons or daughters. Further, as Christians we must beware of any kind of in-group mentality that marginalizes others.

The same God who calls us to family-type community also calls us to treat with genuine hospitality strangers or others not in the community. St. Benedict gave this motto to his monks: *"Hospes venit, Christus venit"*: "When a guest comes, Christ comes." We will know a renewed church not only by its close, committed community interaction among members but also by its hospitality to non-members.

Hospitality can be difficult because many people are shy and fearful of meeting new people. Hospitality takes effort, and strangers who may themselves also be shy may rebuff our overtures. Nevertheless, hospitality is an important part of Christian service, both among members and to non-members. Hospitality plays a major role in evangelizing new people, attracting others to the church and to our Christian communities.

In Acts 10:37-43 Peter summarizes for the Gentiles the gospel that had been given to the Jews. These verses pick out the high points of Luke's Gospel. The Good News proper begins when God anoints Jesus of Nazareth with the Holy Spirit and power. We could easily overlook that anointing when we read Luke 3:21-22 among Luke's 24 chapters, but Luke, through Peter, here reminds us that his anointing by the Spirit grounds Jesus' entire mission. Peter summarizes Jesus' work and places special emphasis on his exorcisms. The apostle gives particular witness to what Jesus did and suffered and to the fact that God raised him from the dead.

The rest of Peter's speech in Acts 10 continues the good news about Jesus. This adaptation of the gospel message for the Gentiles emphasizes Jesus, not as Jewish Messiah, but as judge at the last judgment. Early Christian preaching to pagans strongly emphasized that sinners would face judgment for their behavior. To startle sinners from their complacency, the first Christians did include a little "fire and brimstone" in their evangelizing sermons.

In America especially, Catholics have tended to be put off by the stern approach of revivalists and by the alleged emphasis on hell and punishment in Catholic teaching before Vatican II. Yet even though Christian faith and behavior do not originate primarily from fear of hell, the early church did preach judgment for sin. Has the pendulum swung too far in recent decades? Is it truly good pastoral practice to preach almost *exclusively* about God's love, without ever mentioning that God hates sin? Jesus certainly mentioned hell in his preaching. If we are faithful to his message, can we totally avoid causing fear or pain?

Sometimes people simply will not change without fear or pain. Only fear or pain will motivate some of them to go to see a doctor when they are sick. Alcoholics will often not seek healing until they have hit rock bottom. Many smokers seem unable to quit smoking until their doctor tells them that they must either quit or die. Several ex-smokers have told me that when faced with that choice, their decision was easy! Similarly, sometimes the only way in which to jolt unrepentant sinners out of their complacency is to instill a little fear of death or hell into them.

The proverb "The fear of the Lord is the beginning of wisdom" (Prv 9:10) relates to giving people warnings. Often preachers almost do away with the reference to fear in this proverb by stressing exclusively that the Hebrew word signifies religious reverence. However, the Old Testament has many passages about people who repent under the threat of God's wrath and punishment for their wrongdoing. The proverb does not say that fear of the Lord (in the sense of real fear of his punishment) is *enough* for wisdom, but that it is its beginning.

A New Testament proverb says that perfect love casts out fear (1 Jn 4:18). There is no contradiction between the two proverbs. A state of perfect love indeed casts out fear, but perfect love already implies Christian maturity. For people whose love is immature and imperfect and who tend to compromise in their morality, fear of hell can be a deterrent to sin as well as a beginning of wisdom. We need to recall God's judgment occasionally in order to warn people not to try to take advantage of God's forgiveness. God is not mocked.

The mention of judgment in Acts 10 leads to the offer of forgiveness. To the receptive Gentiles, the Holy Spirit comes as he did at Pentecost (Acts 10:44-48). Once again, God reaches out to forgive and cleanse sinners. We need not fear God if we are open to receiving God's forgiveness and to changing our behavior with God's help. Scripture often shows that God seeks us out in love even when we are in our sins (e.g., Rom 5:8).

Disputes and the Council of Jerusalem—Acts 15

Acts 15 provides a very helpful precedent for settling disputes and dissensions within the church. Although in Acts 11 Peter had convinced the mother church in Jerusalem, other Jewish Christians were still upset about baptizing pagans without circumcision. Ordinary Christians do not always easily accept changes by their leaders.

Some Jewish Christians went to the church in Antioch, which was baptizing pagans, and objected. When Paul and Barnabas disputed with them over the issue of circumcision, the Antioch church sent them and those who were raising objections to Jerusalem to settle the case before the apostles and elders there. Even among good Christians, some arguments are inevitable. When disputes cannot be settled on a local level, Acts 15 exemplifies how to take them to a council of church leaders.

After this council at Jerusalem, Christianity has had many councils among leaders of the universal church. Councils, where Christians on opposing sides of issues can settle their differences in debate, are the New Testament way to solve disputes. In recent church history, however, disputes often tragically lead the opposed factions into schism. Christians can disagree over fundamental issues and yet remain unified if they agree to settle their disputes before leaders and to abide by common agreements.

How was the dispute in Acts 15 settled? First, both sides presented their views. Then came considerable debate. Peter gave witness to how God had changed his heart and mind on the issue. He argued from his experience, and added theological arguments. His clinching theological argument was that God saves both Jews and Gentiles through the grace of Jesus. God saves us by making us holy through his Holy Spirit, which we receive by faith and not by any works we can perform.

Then Paul and Barnabas bore witness to the good fruits of their work among the Gentiles. God had performed signs and wonders through them among the Gentiles and thus confirmed their mission. We test an approach by its fruits. Does it have good results? Does it lead people closer to God? Are there any negative results from it? The second major factor influencing the church's decision in Acts 15 was the positive fruit borne by the approach of Paul and Barnabas to the Gentiles.

The third and decisive factor in the decision of the council came from James, who by this time seems to have become the head of the local Jerusalem church (cf. also Acts 12:17). James settles the argument with Scripture, confirming from the Bible Peter's experience. Scripture had already predicted that God was calling the Gentiles as well as the Jews to himself. Thus, Amos 9:11-12 had prophesied that God would restore the fallen house of David "that the rest of men may seek the Lord, and all the Gentiles who *are called* by my name" (Acts 15:17). However unexpected this turn to the Gentiles may have been to the first Jewish Christians, Scripture had long ago foretold it.

Therefore, the church could trust these developments. Christians should not make it difficult for the Gentiles to turn to God. Conversion was traumatic enough for pagans, who risked expulsion from their families for joining this new cult.

The church decided that pagans should not have to adopt the entire Jewish culture, since God had already given his Holy Spirit to them as non-Jews.

This model is critically important for evangelizing new peoples from different cultures today. God has given his Holy Spirit to Africans as he has to Western Europeans and Americans. We should not force Africans to take on our western culture when they accept Christianity. We need to find forms of expressing Christianity that adapt as much as possible to their cultures. The same is true for Oriental and other peoples.

Whenever two cultures meet, some compromises will always be necessary. Because the first Christians shared community meals and held Eucharist in meal settings, James asked the Gentile Christians to abstain from meat that had been sacrificed to idols or that had been prepared in a non-kosher way (strangled or with blood in it). These three kosher regulations enabled Jewish and Gentile Christians to have shared Eucharistic communities.

Christianity transcends any one cultural expression; it embraces many cultures, peoples, and ways of doing things. To spread the complete gospel today, we must be willing to relinquish some things we may previously have considered important, once we are sure that to do so is compatible with Scripture and church teaching. Christianity is inclusive of all cultures, but it also challenges each of them, including our own.

The gospel, for instance, condemns American styles of material consumption, individualism, sexual immorality, unbridled competition, exploitation of weaker nations, and warlike attitudes. Living as a Christian requires changes in those American values that are incompatible with the gospel. Although Christians try to inculturate their practices and adapt to different cultures, Christianity always retains also a countercultural impact. Through their disputes, discussion, concessions, and agreement, the early Christians in Acts 15 exemplify a way in which to achieve this balance.

NINE

The Call and Mission of Paul, God's Servant

Luke devotes almost two-thirds of the Acts of the Apostles to Paul, the traveling apostle, a very special model for us. Paul demonstrates for us how to be a witness to Christ and a servant of God on our Christian way. We shall examine especially the three versions of Paul's call in Acts 9, 22, and 26. We shall consider Paul as a model for evangelization, Paul's farewell advice to the later church in Acts 20, and the witness he gave through his suffering until the finale in Rome in Acts 21–28.

A Light to Gentiles—Acts 9, 22, 26

Paul's conversion is a crucial story that Acts repeats twice for emphasis. It is helpful to compare all three versions. They contain several small variations in details around a stable core. For example, in one version Paul's companions only hear the voice but do not see anyone (Acts 9:7). In another, they see the light with Paul but do not hear the voice (22:8-9; cf. 26:13-14).

Apparently Luke is unconcerned by such inconsistencies among his three versions of Paul's call. The authors of New Testament narratives, such as the Gospels and Acts, spontaneously and deliberately adapt their accounts to their situations and audiences. They stress what is relevant to their readers, and pass over what does not concern them. The three versions of

Paul's conversion are addressed to different audiences: the readers directly (Acts 9), the Jews at Jerusalem (Acts 22), and King Agrippa and the Roman governor (Acts 26). Rather than read more into such differences than the writers themselves did, let us focus on what God is saying to us as we read or pray through each account.

The nucleus of all three versions of Paul's call is that on the way to Damascus, Jesus "turned Paul around," as the word "conversion" literally means. This turnaround was so abrupt and so unexpected that the Jerusalem Christians had to be reassured that Paul was now in fact on their side. Only after Barnabas vouched for him did they feel safe in his presence (9:27-28).

Jesus' call to Paul changed his life dramatically. Luke describes Paul's call using the same traditional form that the Bible used for the calls of Moses and the prophets. Just as God had called them by name in a special way and changed their lives, so he now calls Paul by name.

When God calls us, he addresses us also by name. God may call us by name twice, with insistence: "Saul, Saul," "Moses, Moses," "Samuel, Samuel." He catches our attention when we otherwise might not hear him calling us. Sometimes we do not recognize God's voice, and mistake him for someone else. Thus, Samuel thought his master Eli was calling him, until, after the third call, Eli realized that the speaker was God. Finally, after the fourth call, Samuel was ready to respond, "Speak, Lord, for your servant is listening" (1 Sm 3:8-10).

Sometimes we are preoccupied with concerns of this world, so that God must cast us to the ground and call, "Saul, Saul." Sometimes he must attract our curiosity and induce us to investigate what some marvelous sign means. Then he can summon us from the burning bush, "Moses, Moses!" (Ex 3:4).

At times God has to repeat his call to us because we really do not want to hear it. We would rather not acknowledge the gnawing realization that God may be asking something of us. Like Martha, busy about many things, we distract ourselves instead of coming to Jesus' feet and listening, as did Mary. However, God continues to call out to us in various ways: through Scripture, through events, through people, and, on the occasions when we are sufficiently quiet, through prayer.

We often have reasons for wanting to avoid God's call to us. We are anxious about what God may want to say to us. We realize that some things in our lives are not right, but we do not want to give them up. Therefore, Jesus' call to Paul begins with a rebuke: "Saul, Saul, why do you persecute me?" To us he might say:

Why do you neglect me in your brothers and sisters?
Why do you take advantage of me in your workers?
Why do you exclude me from your love?
Why do you treat me as a sexual object in your girlfriend or boyfriend?
Why do you refuse to forgive me in someone who has wronged you?

Jesus reminds us that what we do to others we do to him. Saul was certainly not aware that he was persecuting Jesus himself, only that he was persecuting Christians.

The heavenly speaker is familiar with Saul, but Saul does not know who the speaker is, so he replies, "Who are you, Lord?" Saul's manner of addressing the speaker indicates his awareness that the one speaking has authority, but Saul does not yet recognize his voice. God also calls us before we even know him. As we respond to his call, we begin to learn who he is.

In Philippians 3:8, Paul writes that he considers nothing comparable to the overwhelming value of "knowing Christ Jesus my Lord." He wants to know Jesus as Jesus knows him. Paul wants knowledge of the heart, the knowledge of lovers, not mere knowledge of the head or catechism answers about who Jesus is. Jesus offers that same knowledge of the heart to us.

Jesus answers Saul's question, "I am Jesus, whom you are persecuting." Saul had known about Jesus. That was why he was persecuting the Christians. He thought they were following a false messiah.

The curse in Deuteronomy 21:23 against individuals who were hanged on a tree kept many Jews, including Saul, from believing in Jesus. They thought that Jesus' crucifixion disproved any claims that he was the Messiah. Sometimes, with the best of intentions, we cannot reconcile what actually happens with how we think God acts. If we struggle with the problem long enough and ask God to reveal the solution to us, we might come to radically new ways of looking at old truths. Thus, after his conversion, Paul had to sort out his confusion about a cursed Messiah.

In Galatians 3:10-14 Paul comes to a radical conclusion. Crucifixion remains the curse he believed it to be, but Jesus took upon himself our curse for disobeying the Law (Dt 27:26). Thus Jesus fulfills the role of the suffering servant in Isaiah 53, who bore our transgressions and took upon himself our punishment. We need not dread the punishment due for our sins because Jesus has already taken it upon himself on our behalf.

Paul's blindness for three days reminds us of the disciples' confusion in Luke 24 between the discovery of the empty tomb and Jesus' explanation from the Scripture. We can see in Paul's blindness a symbol of our own confusion upon first experiencing God in a new way. As a rule, we cannot fully comprehend what has happened to us.

In Acts 9:10-19 a disciple called Ananias cannot understand how Jesus could have chosen Saul the persecutor. Yet Jesus replies that Paul "is a chosen instrument of mine to carry my name before the Gentiles and kings and the sons of Israel" (9:15). Jesus makes surprising choices of followers, such as Saul the persecutor or us. He chooses even us as instruments to carry his name before others.

We may not feel worthy, or others may not think we are worthy. But, for his own reasons, God nevertheless chooses us. No matter how great a persecutor, sinner, or unbeliever we may have been, God can cleanse, purify, and transform us into his chosen instruments. False humility or guilt should not prevent us from answering God's call.

Saul bears witness to Jews and Gentiles about what he has seen and heard. His witness is not to hearsay, but to his personal experience. In this, Paul is a model for us in our Christian way. Every Christian, no matter how apparently insignificant, is called to be a witness to Jesus as Christ, Lord, and Son of God. However, we cannot credibly bear witness to what we have not ourselves seen and heard. Christian witness requires personal experience of God and of his love, forgiveness, healing, and help. Personal experience imparts authority to our preaching and teaching about God.

Like Paul, we are all called to bear witness to how Jesus has touched our lives. Such witness can be the most powerful means of evangelization, but not all attempts to give witness are helpful. We should not force our testimony on unwilling listeners.

We should not nag family members or spouses to try our forms of prayer or religious experience, or even to appreciate them. Paul demonstrates to us that testimony should focus on Christ, not on ourselves. Testimonies to healing should focus on the healing, not on the sickness or problem. Some testimonies degenerate into serious criticisms of a person's spouse or of someone else. We need to purify the way in which we give witness, so that we indeed give glory to God and attract others to him.

In Acts 9:15-16, our Lord told Ananias not only that Paul would be his witness before all peoples, but that he would have to suffer much for Jesus' name. We cannot be witnesses unless we are willing to suffer. Fear is the greatest obstacle to Christian witness. Willingness to suffer for Jesus' name confronts fear head on. No one can deter us from telling about Jesus if we are not afraid of what people think of us or of rejection.

In Acts 21-26, Paul suffers a great deal in bearing witness to Jesus. He is called before courts to defend his integrity and faith. He survives beatings, imprisonment, and attempts to kill him, but nothing forces Paul to be silent about Jesus. Paul's example challenges us all to witness fearlessly to Jesus, no matter what the cost.

Peter and Paul: The Christian Way Is Consistent

The Acts of the Apostles emphasize parallels between Peter and Paul. Both heal the lame, raise the dead, confront Jewish authorities, and convert Gentiles. Paul's sermon in Acts 13 sounds very much like Peter's in Acts 2. Both preach the same message and perform similar signs and wonders. Both do everything in Jesus' name, and give all the credit and glory to Jesus.

Luke does not stress the uniqueness of Peter and Paul as persons, but rather what they have in common as eyewitnesses and ministers of God's Word and healing. We too should not focus on human ministers of God's grace but on God himself. We should not say, "I belong to Paul," or "I belong to Cephas" (1 Cor 1:12-13), but "I belong to Christ!" Some people who have been powerful instruments in my own conversion have since left the church. That does not make my own conversion any less valid or lasting. God is the one who acts through his ministers in our lives, and God should be our focus.

Paul: A Model for Evangelization

Paul's missionary work provides us with a pattern for evangelizing: by bearing witness and preaching; by founding communities for the new Christians; by providing pastoral oversight for those communities in person, by letters, through helpers like Timothy, and through local elders he ordains; then by journeying onward to preach and found new communities. Personal testimony and preaching convert people to Christ. Communities provide necessary follow-up and nurture the new Christians to further growth and maturity. Therefore, Paul founds churches wherever he converts numbers of people.

Acts illustrates how Paul guided those churches personally when present, and through helpers like Timothy and Silas when absent. Paul's letters also demonstrate that he sent letters when he could not personally be with a church. After he left the churches he had founded to evangelize new areas, he ordained elders to exercise pastoral care as local leaders.

In the late twentieth century, when Pentecostalism and charismatic renewal were particularly popular, wandering preachers and evangelists would often come to a city, preach, and convert numbers of people, then leave town without having made any provision for those whom they had converted. Most new converts are vulnerable to falling back into their old sins. Without further growth and teaching and without support to withstand habitual temptations, their last state can be worse than their first. It is irresponsible to convert people without providing them with a community in which to grow in their faith.

Paul too was a wandering evangelist, but not like the ones described above. He stayed in a city long enough to lay the groundwork and to set up structures for a local church community. He did not leave his new converts unsupported and exposed to the wiles of the world, the flesh, and the devil.

Paul's evangelization included subsequent teaching by word and example. It included his living with new converts until he could form them into communities and train some local leaders to take care of them after he left. He kept contact with churches he had founded by sending assistants to check on their growth and to help them with difficulties. He wrote letters answering their questions and giving them further instructions for meeting new situations and problems. Evangelization must include some responsibility for the development of those converted.

Contemporaneous with twentieth-century wandering evangelists were traveling Christian "healers" who preached and held healing prayer services and "delivered people from evil spirits" from city to city. Such itinerant Christian healers have responsibilities, similar to those of evangelists, to provide follow-up in their ministry. Healings and deliverance from evil spirits often open up a Pandora's box of previously suppressed memories and pain. Those who have been healed or delivered need further healing, support, and instruction in order to deal with the new problems that arise after the initial healing.

After healings, people also often need advice in adjusting to their new situations. We need to instruct them, for example, not to throw away their medicine until their doctor has certified that they are indeed healed and no longer need it. We also need to show people how to change the patterns of behavior that create the opportunities for spiritual oppression or that lead to sickness.

We must support those who have been healed as they try to break old harmful habits such as overeating, self-pity, drunkenness, uncontrolled anger, resentment, and negative thoughts about themselves or others. We need to encourage them to try again when they fail. We need to show them our own love and God's love and assure them that their healing is real. We should help them learn to trust God and to abandon their anxieties.

We must also provide counseling to assist those who are upset because they have apparently not been healed. We guide them in working through their disappointment and coming to peace with the way in which God is acting in their lives. It is irresponsible to hold healing services in city after city with no follow-up provision for those who attend. There should at least be references to local resources for any who may need further help.

On the other hand, Paul provides an example of what to do once a church has been solidly established and is flourishing on its own. We do not bask in our past accomplishments or seek praise and admiration from people we have helped. Forgetting what lies behind, we move on to God's next task. We are on the Christian way, which is a journey that does not cease until we have reached the promised land of heaven. We continue to win new people for Christ; we do not settle in to enjoy the company of those whom we have already helped.

Paul shows us the meaning of zeal, a virtue that our church recently wounded by clerical scandals quite desperately needs. He embodies a hunger and thirst to tell others the Good News. He exemplifies a burning desire that more and more people be converted or reconciled to God. He sacrifices himself and his own convenience in a single-minded drive to serve others. Nothing deters him, not rejections, persecutions, beatings, shipwrecks, sickness, or dangers of any sort (cf. especially 2 Corinthians).

Paul has consecrated his life to celibacy so that he does not need to divide his attention or limit his evangelizing even to care for a family. He will not settle down and give up from bringing others to know Christ as he does. He never says he has done enough, but brings Christ to others until God says "enough" and takes him home to himself.

Paul's zeal originates in his profound love for Jesus. He loves Jesus so fully that he is willing to pay any price to work for him or to bring others to him. Thus he serves his Lord with extraordinary single-mindedness, letting go of everything he had formerly counted as important (Phil 3:7-11).

Everything else is meaningless in comparison to Paul's knowing his Lord Jesus. For Jesus' sake, Paul gave up all his credentials as a pharisaic rabbi, in order that he might gain Christ and be found in him. He abandoned any claim of his own to righteousness, in order to depend on faith in Christ. Paul was willing and even eager to share in Jesus' lot completely, even in his sufferings. In this way he hoped to share in his glory. Such zealous love and willingness to suffer for Jesus mark a true servant of God.

Paul's Farewell Advice—Acts 20

All of us reach a time in our Christian journey when we must leave our earthly work. We must let go of our ministry and pass it on to others who will follow after us. We need to trust that what we have built will not be destroyed or wasted. Even if we fear it may be, we must surrender our hold on any community we may have formed or any children we may have reared. All parents must let go of their children, freeing them to live their own lives and to make their own mistakes. Letting one's children go is often painful, as when grown children make choices that grieve their parents. The same is true of a founder of a church or religious order or any community. Paul's farewell speech is a model for the way in which to let go our ministry as we reach the end of our role and task on earth.

In Acts 20:18-35, Paul says goodbye to the leaders he has installed to replace him at Ephesus. He recalls his example of the way in which to lead the church. He reminds them, and us, that leaders must lead primarily by example. Leaders are to imitate Paul in serving the Lord humbly despite all trials. No fears or tests should deflect us from serving Jesus by faithfully handing on the truth to our community.

Like Paul, we should not shrink from declaring what is most helpful to our hearers, both to the assembled group and to individuals privately. In the decades since the 1970s, several generations of Catholics have not had the complete message preached or taught to them. Very little has been said about sin, about our need to be saved by Christ, or about our need for repentance and the sacrament of reconciliation. It is important to restore proclamation of the "unabridged" fundamental gospel that calls people to a repentant return to God and to faith in our Lord Jesus Christ. Today, many people do not want to hear about repentance, but we must hand on all that we have been given.

Paul is also an example to us of selfless leadership. He does not care what he must suffer as long as he accomplishes the mission the Lord gave him. He declares that he has done all he could for the community, not holding back any of the gospel. Now the responsibility to live the gospel is the community's.

As disciples today, we must hold fast to what we have received from the apostles. Teachers and leaders are to pass on the truth, refuting the many falsehoods held both by members and non-members of the community. For decades, wolves have come among the flock, ravaging Christians with false teachings about faith and morals.

Especially in this time of scandal and uncertainty, bishops must more fully live up to their responsibility. They must protect the flock from further confusion by pointing out when someone is teaching error. They cannot worry about unpopularity or outrage from the press, even some of the Catholic press.

Finally, Paul is a model for us as he surrenders any possible possessiveness toward churches or communities. Like Paul, we commend our congregation or our children to God's care. We have been only stewards acting in God's name. We have been only servants hired to shepherd God's flock.

The church is God's, not ours. We cannot cling to the people we have helped because ultimately they are God's responsibility. In caring for them, we have simply been working for God. Therefore, like Paul we are not to expect silver or covet any reward from the flock itself for leading it.

God will reward us when he takes us home to him. We do

not make the people we help beholden to us. We do not take advantage of their gratitude by currying from them special favors, privileges, and gifts. Rather, we should earn our own keep so that we, too, can provide for those in need.

The prayer of St. Ignatius Loyola for generosity sums up this attitude well:

Lord, teach me to be generous. Teach me to give and not to count the cost, to fight and not to heed the wounds, to toil and not to seek for rest, to labor and not to ask for reward, save that of knowing I am doing your most holy will.

"It is more blessed to give than to receive" (Acts 20:35c).

The Grand Finale at Rome—Acts 28

Despite all obstacles, God fulfills his promises if we persevere in our mission and in the Christian way. We must sometimes cling to his promises in blind trust when events seem to threaten their fulfillment. Thus Paul reaches Rome despite being shipwrecked and bitten by a snake. Jesus had assured him that he would bear witness at Rome, so that Paul maintains his courage no matter how bleak things look during the storm at sea (Acts 27:23-25).

Luke does not end the Acts of the Apostles with Paul's death but with his preaching "openly and unhindered" (Acts 28:31), that is, on a high note of hope. The unconquered Word of God has spread from Jerusalem well on its way to the ends of the earth, as Jesus had foretold (Acts 1:8). Nothing can stop the progress of God's work.

At the end of Acts, the stage has been set for the church in the time after the apostles. God has fulfilled all the prophecies, except that of the end of the world. We are now living in the final days when the Holy Spirit has been poured out to guide and empower us. As we learn to steep ourselves in God's Word, we, like Paul, can continue our Christian way in hope, no matter what adversity we face.

At the beginning of the third millennium, we continue to find ourselves in the situation envisaged at the end of Acts. The God who makes sterile women pregnant and raises the dead to life chooses us as his servants, empowering us with his Holy Spirit to restore his bride, the church. Like Jesus, Mary, and the apostles, we must be open to God's power breaking into our lives and submit ourselves to his unexpected ways. As we imitate Scripture, the pages of our own lives—just as the Gospel of Luke and Acts—will speak of the constancy of God's love. God wants us in our littleness to say "Yes" to him. Then we can become his hands and arms as he reaches through history to embrace his people.

Notes

Introduction

1. Already in 1978, a symposium sponsored by the U.S. Bishops' Committee on Charismatic Renewal and the Diocesan Liaisons to Charismatic Renewal recommended and described this kind of Bible teaching. See George Martin, ed., *Scripture and the Charismatic Renewal: Proceedings of the Milwaukee Symposium December 1-3, 1978* (Ann Arbor, Mich.: Servant, 1979), especially ch. 5, "Summary and Conclusion," by James A. O'Brien, pp. 106–8.

2. Ibid.

3. An increasing number of scholars have been calling for an approach to Scripture that moves beyond individual passages and books to their meaning within the overall biblical revelation. They refer to this approach as "canonical criticism," because it reads biblical books as part of the whole canon or defined list of Scripture. Professor Brevard S. Childs of Yale has been an early primary proponent of this approach, and he lists others in his pioneering book, *Introduction to the Old Testament as Scripture* (Philadelphia: Fortress, 1979).

4. See George T. Montague, "Hermeneutics and the Teaching of Scripture," the presidential address of the Catholic Biblical Association in *The Catholic Biblical Quarterly* 41 (1979) 1–17, reprinted with minor changes in *Scripture and Charismatic Renewal,* pp. 77–95. Cf. especially notes pp. 123–126, and the authors cited. Compare also the discussion among scholars summarized by Raymond E. Brown, *The Critical Meaning of the Bible* (New York: Paulist, 1981), especially ch. 2, "What the Biblical Word Meant and What It Means."

5. A recent resurgence of scholarly interest in patristic inter-
pretation and in spiritual senses of Scripture has provided
some of the stimulus for this second edition. See, for example, Peter S. Williamson, *Catholic Principles for Interpreting
Scripture: A Study of the Pontifical Biblical Commission's*
The Interpretation of the Bible in the Church (preface by
Albert Vanhoye; Chicago: Loyola, 2001). Additional impe-
tus came from Luke Timothy Johnson and William S. Kurz,
*The Future of Catholic Biblical Scholarship: A Constructive
Conversation* (Grand Rapids, Mich.: Eerdmans, 2002), a
call for Catholic scholars to move further than they ordi-
narily do beyond academic criticism toward interpreting the
Bible for the Church. I also wish to express special gratitude
to the editorial staff of Servant Publications for republishing
this book, and to a retired friend, Fr. William E. Dooley,
S.J., for his generous assistance in revising the manuscript.

Chapter Five
The Cost of Salvation to Jesus and the Disciples

1. C.S. Lewis's *Great Divorce* (New York: Macmillan, 1946)
vividly portrays such choices by people from hell who refuse
to go to heaven because they would first have to admit that
they were wrong. Hell entails that people remain closed in
on themselves, hating God and everyone else. They choose
themselves instead of God, and God honors their choice. As
Lewis puts it, "There are only two kinds of people in the
end: those who say to God, 'Thy will be done,' and those
to whom God says, *'Thy* will be done'" (*Divorce*, p. 72).

Chapter Six
Jesus' Way Leads to Passion and to Victory

1. Matthew and Dennis Linn, *Healing Life's Hurts: Healing Memories Through Five Stages of Forgiveness* (New York: Paulist, 1978).

Chapter Seven
Pentecost: Power for Mission and Community

1. Pope John XXIII used this prayer in convoking Vatican Council II. "Divine Spirit, renew your wonders in this our age as in a new Pentecost, and grant that your Church, praying perseveringly and insistently with one heart and mind together with Mary, the Mother of Jesus, and guided by blessed Peter, may increase the reign of the Divine Savior, the reign of truth and justice, the reign of love and peace. Amen." The quotation is from Gerald T. Farrell, M.M., and George W. Kosicki, C.S.B., *The Spirit and the Bride Say "Come": Mary's Role in the New Pentecost* (Asbury, New Jersey: AMI, 1981), p. ix.

2. Cf. *Catechism of the Catholic Church*, rev. ed. (Vatican City: Libreria Editrice Vaticana, 1997), Part I, Section 1, Chap. 2, Art. 2 "The Transmission of Divine Revelation," § 74-100.

3. Cf. Daniel 12:2 and 2 Maccabees 7:9-11, 14, 23, 29.

Chapter Eight
The Christian Way Is for All Peoples

1. Especially since the Catholic charismatic renewal in the 1970s, many priests and Christian counselors have encountered people suffering from spiritual oppression that seems perhaps exacerbated by their involvement in the occult. From experience, these counselors have learned the danger of dismissing occult practices and the reality of evil spirits in a rationalistic way as harmless foolishness or mere personifications of evil respectively. Matthew and Dennis Linn, *Deliverance Prayer: Experiential, Psychological, and Theological Approaches* (New York: Paulist, 1981) provide an early Catholic charismatic perspective on this matter. The chief exorcist of the Diocese of Rome, Fr. Gabriele Amorth, has two recent accounts (to be read with some discrimination): *An Exorcist Tells His Story* (San Francisco: Ignatius, 1999) and *An Exorcist: More Stories* (San Francisco: Ignatius, 2002).

2. Regarding the example of homosexuality, an early but genuinely compassionate and still helpful book is Leanne Payne, *The Broken Image: Restoring Personal Wholeness Through Healing Prayer* (Westchester, Ill.: Cornerstone, 1981). The most accessible treatment of homosexuality by official church teaching authority is the *Catechism of the Catholic Church* § 2357–59 (plus its context within the meaning of human sexuality, § 2331–36, and the vocation to chastity § 2337–50). A key recent official Catholic document is *On the Pastoral Care of Homosexual Persons*, by the Congregation for the Doctrine of the Faith (Boston: Saint Paul Books & Media, [1986]). For a personal testimony,

see David Morrison, *Beyond Gay* (introduction by Archbishop Charles J. Chaput; Huntington, Ind.: Our Sunday Visitor, 1999). Fr. John F. Harvey, the founder of "Courage," a twelve-step approach to chastity among homosexuals, has written two encouraging books: *The Homosexual Person: New Thinking in Pastoral Care* (San Francisco: Ignatius, 1987), and *The Truth About Homosexuality: The Cry of the Faithful* (San Francisco: Ignatius, 1996). For a set of very recent essays, see *Same-Sex Attraction: A Parent's Guide*, ed. Fr. John F. Harvey and Gerard V. Bradley (San Francisco: Ignatius, 2002).